Comments on other *Amazing Stories* from readers & reviewers

*"You might call them the non-fiction response to Harlequin romances: easy to consume and potentially addictive."*
Robert Martin, *The Chronicle Herald*

*"Tightly written volumes filled with lots of wit and humour about famous and infamous Canadians."*
Eric Shackleton, *The Globe and Mail*

*"This is popular history as it should be... For this price, buy two and give one to a friend."*
Terry Cook, a reader from Ottawa, on **Rebel Women**

*"Stories are rich in description, and bristle with a clever, stylish realness."*
Mark Weber, *Central Alberta Advisor,* on **Ghost Town Stories II**

*"The resulting book is one readers will want to share with all the women in their lives."*
Lynn Martel, *Rocky Mountain Outlook,* on **Women Explorers**

*"*[The books are] *long on plot and character and short on the sort of technical analysis that can be dreary for all but the most committed academic."*
Robert Martin, *The Chronicle Herald*

*"A compelling read. Bertin...has selected only the most intriguing tales, which she narrates with a wealth of detail."*
Joyce Glasner, *New Brunswick Reader,* on **Strange Events**

*"The heightened sense of drama and intrigue, combined with a good dose of human interest is what sets* Amazing Stories *apart."*
Pamela Klaffke, *Calgary Herald*

# AMAZING STORIES®

# STRANGE EVENTS OF ONTARIO

*Enjoy*
*Maria Da Silva*

*Enjoy the Chills*

*Andrew Hind*

# AMAZING STORIES®

# STRANGE EVENTS OF ONTARIO

## Chilling Tales of Phantoms, Curses, and Hauntings

MYSTERY/HISTORY

by Andrew Hind & Maria da Silva

PUBLISHED BY ALTITUDE PUBLISHING CANADA LTD.
1500 Railway Avenue, Canmore, Alberta T1W 1P6
www.altitudepublishing.com
www.amazingstories.ca
1-800-957-6888

Extreme care has been taken to ensure that all information presented in
this book is accurate and up to date. Neither the author nor the
publisher can be held responsible for any errors.

| Publisher | Stephen Hutchings |
| Associate Publisher | Kara Turner |
| Editors | Dianne Smyth and Margaret Sadler |
| Cover and Layout | Bryan Pezzi |

We acknowledge the financial support of the Government
of Canada through the Book Publishing Industry Development
Program (BPIDP) for our publishing activities.

**Altitude GreenTree Program**
Altitude Publishing will plant twice as many trees as were used
in the manufacturing of this product.

**Library and Archives Canada Cataloguing in Publication**

Hind, Andrew
    Strange events of Ontario / Andrew Hind, Maria da Silva.

(Amazing stories)
Includes bibliographical references.
ISBN 1-55439-061-3

    1. Parapsychology--Ontario. I. Da Silva, Maria II. Title.
III. Series: Amazing stories (Canmore, Alta.)

BF1028.5.C3H56 2006      130'.9713      C2006-900857-4

Printed and bound in Canada by Friesens
2 4 6 8 9 7 5 3 1

Dedicated to Jose da Silva, for always believing in us. Sadly, you're not here to see this work completed, but you'll always be with us in every venture that we take.

# Contents

# Prologue

*Leuantido looked down in horror at the rocky cliff where her brothers had flung the body of her lover. Somewhere in the abyss below lay his corpse. Remembering the terrifying event turned the maiden's stomach and she froze in agony. They had been so happy together and so much in love. But her father, the chief, had forbidden their relationship. Her soul mate was not of high enough status, thus he was deemed not worthy to take Leuantido as his bride.*

*With the wind whipping at her raven hair, the young woman cried until she had no more tears to shed. His death was on her hands. She had convinced her lover that her father would eventually relent and that, until that time, they could continue to meet secretly after dark each night. But they were discovered, and it was her lover who paid the price for their deception.*

*Leuantido, her spirit broken, looked over the cliff's edge, desperately hoping to spot her beloved's body. The rocks below were obscured by a sinister grey fog that was thick and cold, like mist escaping from a grave. But the chilling scene didn't dissuade her from what she was about to do. She could not live another moment without her lover — and if they could only be together in death, so be it.*

*The distraught woman stepped over the precipice. "I'm coming, my love," she whispered, as she fell into the swirling mist below. Leuantido was certain this act would finally end her agony. In truth, it was just the beginning ...*

# Chapter 1
# The Dark Realm of Folklore

In earlier more superstitious times, people believed monsters lurked behind every tree, in every shadow, and below every body of water. These creatures inhabited the dark realm of folklore, and there most remain. Some, however, may be more than manifestations of our fear and fascination. Chilling sightings of these monsters continue well into the modern era, providing evidence — circumstantial though it may be — that mer-beasts, ape-men, and vampire-like monsters may in fact inhabit the shadowy recesses of Ontario's landscape.

## Kempenfelt Kelly

A strange sense of dread welled within David Soules. He tried to give it definition, to place its source, but it slipped away from him, elusive and defiant. There was something not right about the fog-shrouded waters of Kempenfelt Bay that morning. The sheep he and his brother James were tending along the shores of Lake Simcoe seemed to sense it also, for they were unusually skittish.

Then, fear mingled with horror as a shadowy form emerged from the depths, a creature distorted and grotesque, unlike anything Soules had ever seen before. "It was a huge long thing that went through the water like a streak ... having huge fin-like appendages, and being very large and very ugly looking." Then, as suddenly as it had appeared, the creature slipped beneath the water once more and was gone. The whole experience had lasted mere moments, but it haunted Soules for a lifetime.

It should be noted that David Soules, like fur-trader witnesses before him, was no newcomer to the wilderness. Indeed, he had a distinguished record serving on the frontiers during the War of 1812, and had extensive nautical experience on the rivers and lakes of Upper Canada. This was not the kind of man who might mistake a beaver or a moose for a sea monster.

This was the first detailed sighting of the lake creature that later became known as Kempenfelt Kelly, among other names. The creature's current and most common name was adopted in 1967 when Arch Brown, a native of Oro-Medonte Township, decided Lake Simcoe's resident sea monster needed a catchier name to go with modern times. He copyrighted the name Kempenfelt Kelly and donated it to the City of Barrie for tourism promotion, putting a cuddly face on the elusive creature.

For hundreds of years, the rarely cuddly mer-beast has been seen across the entire length of Lake Simcoe, from Cooks Bay in the south to the narrows at Orilla in the north. This is the deepest part of the lake, so it's perhaps natural that a creature attempting to elude discovery would reside here. In fact, local lore suggests that there are underwater tunnels beneath Kempenfelt Bay (thus the name) that link Lake Simcoe to other large bodies of water in Canada, and perhaps even to Loch Ness in Scotland. This "theory" would conveniently account for the reports of similar aquatic monsters in these widely dispersed lakes, and explain how a genetic pool large enough to support a viable population could exist.

But, while David Soules may have left us the first written eyewitness account, local Native peoples had for centuries believed that a monstrous creature of some sort inhabited the depths of Lake Simcoe. Their name for it was Mishepeshu, and it was a name they uttered only in hushed tones. They believed Mishepeshu to be an angry and murderous spirit, a creature that feasted on human flesh when sufficiently riled. Sometimes appearing as a sea serpent, other times as a lynx, the creature was always identified by the curved horns that adorned its head.

Fur traders, all of whom were experienced woodsmen and not easily rattled, also reportedly saw this strange creature many times throughout the eighteenth century. By the time Soules had his encounter in 1823, Lake Simcoe's sea monster was already a part of European lore.

The creature, as described by these early witnesses and dozens of people since, defies easy classification. It is almost always brown in colour, with a long neck topped by a head resembling that of a dog both in shape and in features. The monster has often been described as a slow swimmer, gliding along at a leisurely pace even when in the presence of humans, and indeed she seems quite curious by nature, willfully surfacing alongside boats or approaching startled people on shore. The largest specimen sighted was estimated to have been only about three and a half metres in length, much smaller than those creatures reputedly inhabiting Loch Ness or even other Canadian lakes.

The original native name never did catch on with the European settlers, so no one objected when the Barrie newspapers of the early 1900s cleverly labelled it the "C monster" in light of the serpent's association with the local Carley family. Thus, one more name was added to the list. The Carleys operated a boat manufacturing business at the foot of Mulcaster Street in Barrie. For years, their wharf was a popular spot for viewing the beast. During a rowing regatta offshore, Carley was reputedly forced off-course when the creature suddenly surfaced in front of his boat.

In 1903, a beast with a "head as big as a dog and with horns" startled a pair of railway detectives who were boating near the Carley wharf. Two years later, three more people saw the serpent in the same vicinity, and gave a surprisingly detailed and credible account. Amazingly, the *Barrie Advance* reported that these sightings were nothing more than the Carley's pet muskrat.

The "C monster" was later given the name Igopogo by Wellington Charles, a native guide, after a sighting that occurred on July 31, 1952. Charles thought the name was appropriate in light of its similarity to other great sea monsters of Canadian lore, namely Lake Okanagan's Ogopogo and Lake Manitoba's Manipogo.

There is, however, a darker side to the creature. One report that surfaced sometime in the late 1800s suggested the sea monster was responsible for the death of a sheep grazing along the shore of Cooks Bay. A startled witness saw the creature spring from the water and snatch its helpless prey in its mouth, then drag the kill into the lake where it was presumably devoured. This tale should take us back to the creature's origins in aboriginal lore, where Mishepeshu was a feared and respected hunter. Perhaps Kempenfelt Kelly isn't as cuddly as we've come to believe.

Nevertheless, the question remains. Is there really a sea monster lurking in the depths of Lake Simcoe? In recent years, there has been some tantalizing evidence indicating that there might well be. In 1978 and again in 1983, sonar scans of the lake's depths captured something — large anomalies — that indicate the presence of a subsurface serpent-like creature.

Without a doubt, the most remarkable recent evidence comes from a video shot in 1991. A cameraman was videotaping a friend racing his boat in Cooks Bay when the craft suddenly broke down. While the boater began repairs, something quietly surfaced a few metres away. At first, the creature rose up out of the water on a long neck and considered the boater. Then, it slowly sank back into the water and peered upward with only the top of its head visible above the surface. A few moments later, it submerged and did not return. Incredibly, the whole episode was captured on film. The quality of the video images is excellent, clearly showing an unusual creature of some kind.

As the debate rages over Kempenfelt Kelly's identity, and even her very existence, the reclusive creature eludes us in the murky depths of Lake Simcoe. It has lurked within these waters for hundreds of years, and may continue to do so for hundreds more.

**Bloody Redcap**
Blanketed with white and glistening under the mid-winter sun, the land was deceptively beautiful and peaceful. But the cold winds that whirled flurries through the barren treetops and over the white-capped waves on Lake Simcoe hinted at winter's cruelty. It was the time of year when culling takes the old, the young, the sick, and the weak. Death came as suddenly and violently as a blizzard.

Lurking behind the shroud of falling snow was a creature that revelled in such death. It sought to quench its thirst for blood and rid itself of its gnawing hunger. This creature, neither living nor dead, thrived on killing and was known to the residents of Thorah Township as "the redcap."

Located on the eastern shores of Lake Simcoe, Thorah Township was settled in the late 1790s and early 1800s by immigrants from the Highlands of Scotland and from Ireland. Most of the immigrants were discharged soldiers or farmers who had been forced off their lands to make room for large-scale sheep grazing.

The early settlers along Lake Simcoe's eastern shore found diversion from their Spartan existence in the legends and tales brought over from their homeland, turning the region into a rich source of paranormal phenomenon. But the redcap, by far, emerges as the most feared entity from this crowded paranormal pack.

In a sense, the settlers brought this evil unto themselves. Along with their dreams and aspirations for a bright future, they also brought with them their tales concerning the dreaded redcap, and ... perhaps ... even the creatures themselves.

Among the first of these settlers was a Scot by the name of Corporal Crawford, a hardy man who had been discharged from the British army due to the loss of an eye in battle. He came to the eastern shores of Lake Simcoe in 1796 to fish, and was duly impressed with the region he found — waters teaming with trout, pike, and muskellunge; dense forests of maple, oak, ash, and pine; and rich soil well-suited to agricultural endeavours. Corporal Crawford resolved to return at a later date and build a home there.

A few years passed, but eventually he did come back, accompanied this time by his wife and their children. The Crawfords became the first European residents in what is today Thorah Township. Unfortunately, the family didn't get to enjoy the bounty of the land for long, as their bright future was cut tragically short in a most gruesome way.

The first winter in their new home was particularly harsh. Snow was thick and heavy and formed deep blankets, the temperatures plummeted to bone-chilling lows, and game was scarce and unusually lean. Food was in short supply, forcing Corporal Crawford to go on extended hunting excursions to feed his family. He did so reluctantly, however, knowing that while he was away his wife and children were left vulnerable to attack by native groups, wolves, or bears. One can imagine the turmoil he endured each time he waved goodbye and turned his back on his family, not knowing whether they would be there when he returned.

For several months, all went well. Each time he came home Crawford found his family well and eagerly awaiting his arrival. So, as he set out on his next hunt, he did so with far less concern than he had previously felt. Sadly, Crawford returned from this trip to a horrifying homecoming. When he approached the clearing, he hollered a greeting, expecting a mob of excited children to race out and to pile themselves into his arms. His call was greeted by silence. Instantly alarmed, he cast aside the deer he had shot and hurried to the isolated cabin. The door hung open, swaying lazily in the frosty air. By now, Crawford knew something was dreadfully wrong, but still nothing could have prepared him for what he found inside. The entire cabin was painted red with blood. Fragments of bone and shredded clothing littered the barren interior. Corporal Crawford's wife and children had been brutally slain. Some believe they were killed by a pack of hungry wolves, but if legend is to be believed, the true culprit was the bloodthirsty redcap.

The evil and vicious redcap was easily the most terrifying thing to emerge from the shared folklore of Scotland and Ireland, lands long known to be grim and violent. In fact, it was likely their destructive pasts that made these lands so appealing to redcaps, since they prefer to live in mountains and hills that have a history of warfare and terrible deeds.

With its powdery-white complexion and leathery weathered skin, a redcap looks like a very old man. Short and stocky, with fiery red eyes, a long white beard, but with only thin wisps of stringy hair upon its head, they are hideous to behold. Despite a skeletal-like appearance, the creature is broad-shouldered and very strong, and its arms end in long sharp eagle-like claws. Atop its head rests a cap stained red with human blood, which it wears as its trademark.

The redcap is remarkably proficient at killing, having perfected its craft to an art over centuries of practice. While its claws are undeniably fearsome, the murderous fiend often wields an oversized weapon, generally a huge scythe, with which it effortlessly cleaves head from body. No mortal, not even the mightiest Highlander, can stand against a redcap in combat and live to tell about it. According to Scottish folklore, the only known defence against its assault is a profound faith in God. On rare occasions, a redcap has been repelled (as vampires are) by the sign of the cross or by a Bible brandished before it.

The source of numerous terrifying tales throughout the nineteenth century, the redcap had become something of a bogeyman in the Lake Simcoe area. It was the subject of dark stories told over a mug of ale, and was used to frighten children gathered around a fire. For one young girl in particular, the redcap was more than just the villain of a tall tale. It was a very real nightmare, not those that inhabit dreams, but the kind born of all the evil that inhabits the world.

It was early one morning when the young girl jerked herself awake. She was trembling, and her legs were tangled in her blanket as though she'd been running in her sleep. Eager to clear her head after a troubled night, the girl inched her way out of the warmth of her bed and slipped noiselessly out of the cabin and into the early morning mist. She loved this time of day, as the woods lay peaceful and silent and the air smelled fresh and new. Normally, the serenity of the woods put her at ease.

Not on this morning. Something felt wrong. There was heaviness in the air that weighed upon her. The mist was damp, but the chill she suddenly felt was of a different nature. It was the bone-gnawing cold of pure evil. Instinctively, she knew she was not alone.

Then she saw it, silhouetted against the grey morning mist. It was hunched and withered with age, but there was an undeniable fearsomeness about it. The girl was transfixed by glowing red eyes that held her in place. Her mind desperately screamed for her to run ... to hide ... to escape! But she was frozen with terror and was sure she was about to die.

The creature approached her. Tears stained her cheeks as a bony finger drew a line across her brow, the sharp nail painfully cutting open her tender young skin. The redcap smiled wickedly with needle-like teeth. Still unable to move, the girl clenched her eyes shut and waited for the end to come. But when long moments passed without anything happening, and when she could no longer feel the creature's hot breath against her face, the girl dared to open her eyes. She was alone. Alive. The redcap had simply blended into the mist and disappeared.

No one knows why the girl survived, and indeed the entire event might be explained away as a particularly vivid nightmare. That's certainly how her parents consoled their daughter and themselves that morning. But two elements make such a hasty dismissal problematic. The first was the butchered sheep found in the fields later that day. Perhaps the handiwork of a wolf, perhaps not. The second, and most convincing, was the deep gash across the girl's forehead. It was abnormally slow in healing, and it remained painfully visible for the rest of her years.

The rural way of life still pervades in the small communities on Lake Simcoe's eastern shores, and tradition remains firmly entrenched. The locals are proud of their ancestry, and of their rich culture. While tales of the redcap are fading, these creatures still haunt the darkest recesses of the imagination. They are still the epitome of violence and terror, another reminder of the troubled past of the settler's ancient lands.

These strange events took place in the 1800s, a time when the shores of Lake Simcoe were still shrouded in the darkness of heavy forest and when people still clung to Old World folklore and superstition. Over the past two centuries, much has changed. Today, Lake Simcoe is a popular recreational destination and much of its surroundings have been heavily developed. The modern world has little room for superstition and folklore, but still ...

**Old Yellow Top**

Reports of a large, hairy, ape-like creature haunting the mining region near Cobalt are numerous and go back more than a century. This beast seems to be a subspecies of the famous Sasquatch, or Bigfoot, of the Pacific Northwest. Large and elusive, the beasts instill both fear and curiosity. Sasquatch are covered in coarse brown hair, have unusually long arms, stand over seven feet in height, and weigh over 300 pounds.

The only apparent difference between the hairy man-ape of northern Ontario and those of the Pacific coast is the light-coloured hair that covers its head, neck, and shoulders. The Ontario creature's nickname, Old Yellow Top, is derived from this distinctive colouration.

The earliest recorded references to the creatures collectively known as Sasquatch are found in the lore of North American Native peoples. To them, there is nothing mythical about the Sasquatch. Though shy, Sasquatch were very much a part of the real world, as much as any other form of wildlife. They were considered dangerous beings, not to be trifled with.

The first written account of the Sasquatch dates back to 1792 at the time of the Spanish explorer, Jose Mariano Mozino, who was travelling through California. He reserved an entire page of his journal for observations of the creature, as related to him by the Native people he encountered. As an experienced explorer who had already seen much that would shake European preconceptions of the world, Mozino accepted the native tales as fact.

David Thompson, the famous explorer, was the first to make reference to Bigfoot in Canada. During his travels through the Rocky Mountains in 1811, Thompson recorded, in his January 5th journal, the warnings of local Native people about a giant hairy man-like creature that inhabited the region. Initially, he was sceptical. However, he was shaken from his self-assurance when, a few days later, he discovered abnormally large, unidentified, and vaguely humanoid foot-prints in the snow. Natives assured him these were the tracks of the Bigfoot. Thereafter, Thompson wasn't nearly so quick to dismiss the existence of the beasts.

Old Yellow Top first emerged from the shroud of myth and folklore in September 1906. The area around Cobalt was then unsettled and the mining frenzy was only in its infancy, so there were few humans in the imposing wilderness. A work crew found itself deep in the woods east of Cobalt building the head-frame of the Violet Mine, when an ape-like being emerged from the forest. The anxious men, who were all convinced that what they beheld was definitely not a bear, watched the creature for several long minutes until its shape blended in with the trees at the edge of the clearing. When the men returned to civilization some time later and told their sensational story, a news-starved media dubbed the creature the Traverspine Gorilla (it was also referred to for a time as the Precambrian Shield Man).

In July 1923, two prospectors, J.A. MacAuley and Lorne Wilson, were taking test samples of their mining claims northeast of Wettlaufer Mine near Cobalt when they saw what initially looked like a bear feasting in a blueberry patch. With courage that bordered on recklessness, Wilson threw a stone at the animal.

To his horror, the creature stood up to an erect seven feet — bared its teeth — and let out a roar of defiance. The sound was ear piercing and dreadful enough to leave the two men trembling in fright. It was like nothing they had ever heard before. Motivated by absolute terror, they fled.

But the details of the creature's appearance remained forever etched in their minds. What they had initially mistaken for a bear was in fact a humanoid in every way similar to the Sasquatch of the Rocky Mountains. Except for one important detail. "Its head was kind of yellow," recounted Lorne Wilson, "and the rest of it was black like a bear, all covered in hair."

Another well-documented sighting took place in April of 1946, near the hamlet of Gillies Depot. It happened in the early morning when a woman and her young son began the long walk along the railway tracks into Cobalt to do the family's weekly shopping. As it was early spring, the woman was wary of stumbling into young bear cubs and their protective mothers. So she reacted very quickly when a large shadow in the periphery of her vision moved toward the tracks. She instantly swept her young son close to her body, using her small frame to shield him from danger. What she then saw shocked and terrified her.

This was no bear, nor was it a wolf, or any other creature she was familiar with. It walked effortlessly on two legs "almost like a man." The woman later described it as more man than beast. She knew instantly that this was the legendary Old Yellow Top. In her panic her mind flew through the stories the miners used to tell about the creature — and she froze to the spot — helpless. But, apparently uninterested in its captive audience, the beast disappeared across the tracks and into the woods on the other side, leaving the considerably shaken woman and her very frightened son to continue on their journey.

The most famous encounter with Old Yellow Top occurred on an August night in 1970, though 27 miners and one bus driver very nearly didn't live to tell about it. That evening had begun normally enough. The sun had long since set and the night was dark and still. Many of the miners dozed lightly on uncomfortable seats, waiting for their long shift to begin at the Cobalt Lode, while driver Aimee Latreille expertly guided the bus along the road through the wilderness. It was a journey he had taken numerous times before, always without incident. This night, however, would be quite different.

The sky was clear and the moon's eerie glow caused the shadows of trees to stretch out across the road like long, dark, clawed fingers. No vehicle disturbed the silence along this isolated stretch of northern Ontario highway, except for the bus carrying miners to the graveyard shift. Suddenly, the piercing beams of the headlights revealed a dark shape emerging from the forest — a large, man-like creature covered entirely in reddish-brown hair — except for a light-coloured mane around its shoulders.

The headlights illuminated the beast's shocking features, so terrifying the bus driver that his flesh began to creep, and he unthinkingly slammed on the brakes and swerved to avoid it. When the bus hit the soft shoulder, Latreille lost control of the vehicle and nearly plunged down a rocky embankment. It was a close call. The creature we now know as Old Yellow Top had almost claimed its first human victims.

It's hard to say exactly what unnerved him more, his near brush with death or the nature of the creature he had almost hit. "At first I thought it was a big bear," Latreille said, "but then it turned to face the headlights and I could see some light hair, almost down to the shoulders. It couldn't have been a bear. I have heard of this thing before but I never believed it. Now I am sure." One of the miners at the front of the bus, a man named Larry Cormack, also caught a brief glimpse of the creature and supported Latreille's report. "It looked like a bear, but it didn't walk like one. It was kind of half-stooped over."

The near-tragic accident brought media attention to Old Yellow Top once again. The *North Bay Nugget* ran the headline — "Ape-like Creature at Large" in its August 5, 1970 edition, and for a while there was intense interest in the Bigfoot of northern Ontario. Since then, however, the beast has been rather elusive and public interest has faded.

Though Old Yellow Top has only been seen sporadically in the last four decades, he may simply be biding his time. After all, sightings have always been rare and fleeting and, considering the remoteness and expanse of the wilderness the creature calls home, it's little wonder. But one thing is for certain. Regardless of the creature's rare appearances, the mystery that surrounds it will always remain.

# Chapter 2
# Ontario's Haunted Inns

any of Ontario's country inns offer warm and welcoming hospitality in historical settings, and it's likely that this appealing combination makes them among the province's most haunted locations. For us, inns represent a temporary home away from home, whether it is for a lovers' getaway or for a retreat from the bustle of everyday life. After a night or two, however, we leave with nothing except memories. But, for the ghostly patrons that haunt these inns, the stay is permanent.

### Chestnut Inn
Strange events and eerie coincidences happen to all of us at one point or another. Sometimes, they can leave you questioning your past, your future, and your sanity. Take the story

of a young woman's experiences at the Chestnut Inn, for example.

It began innocently enough on a warm summer day. Theresa drove to Cookstown with a friend, intent on soaking up the charm of the quaint village and spending a day wandering through antique shops full of timeless treasures. She never expected that, before the day was through, the past would reveal itself to her in a very personal way.

Theresa decided to stop at the Chestnut Inn for lunch. Even 10 years later, she remembers how warm and inviting the restaurant was, with its rustic décor and an old-fashioned bar to one side. After she was seated, a waitress approached and asked Theresa if she'd ever been to the restaurant before. She hadn't. But for some reason the waitress just couldn't take her eyes away from Theresa. It was as if she was uncomfortable with, and yet intrigued by, Theresa's presence.

The reason revealed itself as Theresa was leaving. The waitress stopped her and asked if she had by any chance noticed the picture hanging in the staircase leading to the second floor, because the woman depicted in the grainy Victorian photograph was her spitting image. Theresa hadn't seen the photograph, nor did she have any inclination to. By this time she was more than a little unnerved, and concluded that the waitress was out of her mind.

Years passed before she thought of that incident again. Then one day, just for laughs, Theresa accompanied a friend to a psychic. She was startled when the medium brought up the subject of the Chestnut Inn. The psychic told them about the young woman who haunted it — a murdered young woman — who resembled Theresa in uncanny detail.

Theresa decided to return to the inn. Perhaps she could find an answer to this strange coincidence. The building had changed through the years. It now had a small shop where the restaurant used to be, with a charming tearoom, The Princely Pear, in the back. Of course, the staircase remained the same, but by now the picture was long gone. Theresa felt herself drawn to the upstairs, which housed several bed and breakfast rooms, and was guided up the narrow staircase by an employee willing to accommodate her fancy.

Climbing the stairs, Theresa stumbled on the top step. She hadn't caught her foot on anything or taken a misstep. It was almost as if someone — or something — had given her a shove and thrown her off balance. Stranger things followed. When entering one of the bedrooms, Theresa found it some-how familiar. She felt as if she were home, as if she'd been there before. It was an eerie coincidence that most of the furniture in the room was similar to that in her own house. At this point Theresa was feeling confused and a little fright-ened. There were still too many questions left unanswered and too many feelings she couldn't explain. The one thing she was sure of, however, was that something tragic had befallen a woman in that house long ago. She didn't know how she knew. She just knew.

Things began to fall into place not long after. Theresa

was talking to a client, when once again the Chestnut Inn entered the conversation. It was as if she was destined to never forget the place. From her first visit on, despite the passage of years or the distance of kilometres, Theresa had been periodically reminded of the historic restaurant. The tale her client related that day was both uncanny and strangely familiar.

Apparently, several ghosts haunt the Chestnut Inn. The most commonly seen apparition is that of a beautiful young woman, typically seen standing forlornly atop the stairs. The staff has taken to calling this tragic figure "Catherine." No one knows if this was indeed her name, but it was the name that suddenly jumped into the mind of a startled waitress who had just witnessed her sudden manifestation. Catherine, it seems, came from a well-to-do family who, at some point in the late nineteenth century, owned and resided in the building that today houses the Princely Pear Tearoom. Catherine fell hopelessly in love with a dashing young man in town, but her father hated the notion and claimed that the suitor wasn't good enough for his beloved daughter. Father and daughter argued frequently and loudly. It pained Catherine that the two men she loved couldn't both be a part of her life. She refused to choose between them, and continued to see her beloved in secret.

Then, the unthinkable happened. Unwed Catherine was "with child." In Victorian society, a scandal such as this could ruin a family. Her father was furious when he discovered her secret. Everything he had built over his decades in town — the business, his sterling reputation, a position amongst the elite of society — was about to be destroyed by this one selfish act by a daughter who, in his rage-clouded mind, was little more than a tramp. He wouldn't have it. He simply would not be brought down in such a fashion.

One morning, Catherine left her bedroom to go down for breakfast. She was absently rubbing the little belly that contained so much hope for her future, and didn't notice the figure looming behind her. Just as Catherine was about to descend the stairs, she felt a violent push from behind. As she tumbled down the stairs — the last thing she saw was the menacing grin of her murderer — her own father.

Though it was easy enough for Catherine's father to rid himself of scandal, it was not so easy to rid himself of his daughter. A free-spirited soul in life, not one willing to play to conventions, she became even more restless in death.

Not long after her passing, Catherine began appearing again, supernaturally haunting her father as a means of revenge. Her spirit would appear atop the staircase and then re-enact the fatal fall. The frightful sounds of her body tumbling down the stairs nearly drove her father mad with guilt.

And it continued to have the same disturbing effect on the staff and patrons of the Chestnut Inn. Even today, waitresses busy with their tasks in the tearoom will occasionally hear the gut-wrenching sound of someone falling down the staircase. But when they run to investigate, expecting to find someone or something crumpled on the floor, they find nothing at all.

The ghostly Catherine inhabits one of the upstairs bedrooms. On some occasions, passers-by on the street below have seen the figure of a woman in black standing in the window. And sometimes, strange sounds are emitted from this room. One episode in particular stands out in the mind of an unidentified former staff member.

"We were downstairs and you could hear things upstairs. Not just footsteps as we often heard, but other noises as well. Noises we couldn't explain. Creepy noises. When we went up to investigate, we heard a little girl laughing in one of the bedrooms, but as soon as the door opened, the laughter stopped. There was no one there."

Is this laughter the sound of Catherine as a young child, reliving happier times? Or is there, in fact, another ghost in residence at the Chestnut Inn? According to reports, mediums going through the building have sensed as many as 35 ghosts there.

For Theresa, and perhaps many others, the Chestnut Inn is still a mystery, and probably will always remain so.

### Severn River Inn

Without the distractions of the modern world, guests find it easy to relax and unwind at the Severn River Inn. They are transported back to an earlier, simpler time. There are no phones or televisions in the inn's 10 guestrooms, and they'd be out of place in rooms furnished with antiques, brass beds, and heirloom quilts. It's so peaceful, in fact, that over the years some "guests" have refused to check out.

The Severn River Inn is the afterlife home of at least two ghosts. One is that of a little girl, often mischievous and playful, sometimes sad and lonely. The other is that of a former proprietor, most likely the inn's founder. He continues his daily duties unaware of the fact that he is no longer part of our physical world.

Curt and Kaaren Brandt and Norman and Rosalie Rondeau operate the inn today. Both couples readily admit to having experienced a string of unexplained activity, some relatively minor, some downright unsettling. And while they acknowledge that the entities do exist, they've yet to positively identify the spirits or the reasons for their continual haunting.

The ghost of the unnamed little girl is the most active of the out-of-time pair. Rosalie regularly gets tapped on the shoulder in the dining room, while Kaaren has experienced playful tuggings on her coat while raking the leaves in the yard. The sounds of children playing can occasionally be heard in the back stairway. "I hear them running around and playfully squealing," Kaaren says, "but nothing is ever visible and no kids are present."

The antics of this spectral child keep the staff entertained, and occasionally frustrated. Objects frequently go missing at the inn. For example, a special knife used in the kitchen disappeared and was never seen again, as did a piping bag used for decorating cakes. Whispered voices are heard, furniture is moved around, and lights have gone off and on of their own accord.

While the child's ghost has never been seen, the same cannot be said of the former proprietor. Just recently, a staff member went into the basement, only to find that she was standing face to face with an "old-fashioned gentleman" who had a handlebar moustache and wore the clothes of a nine-teenth century shopkeeper. The woman fled upstairs and has since refused to go into the basement alone. Another event occurred several years ago. Kaaren was standing beside the coffee machine when she heard a gentleman greeting her and "the face of an older grey-haired man" flashed before her eyes. She spun around, but found herself completely alone. The owners are convinced this ghost is that of the original owner, Joseph Jackson, who built the inn back in the 1860s.

Jackson has only been seen a few times, but he makes himself heard more often. Gabriella Kira, a chef at the inn, has had a number of experiences. "One evening I was work-ing with Rhonda. It was about eight o'clock and we were the only two people in the inn," she relates in Terry Boyle's *Haunted Ontario*. "We were in the bar area when we heard footsteps upstairs. Then we heard someone walking up and down the stairs by the back dining room stairs leading up to the second floor. The floors creak, so we know someone is walking around. I also heard a door slam. It sounded like either Room 3 or 4." Understandably, neither woman volunteered to investigate the mysterious noises.

Another time, Gabriella and Norman were alone in the building after it had closed for the evening. Gabriella was in the basement taking some food out of the freezer for the next day when she heard the distinct sound of someone walking around in the bar area. She thought perhaps it was Norman, but she came upstairs to find him still on the second floor. He hadn't moved from his desk there. Gabriella admits to being a little spooked by the experience.

It's not just the owners and their staff who have run-ins with the supernatural. Guests likewise witness strange things at the inn. One autumn night a few years back, a married couple was staying at the inn. They spent the days driving the backroads of Muskoka, enjoying the spectacular fall foliage for which the region is famed. Exhausted from their explorations, and upon returning to the inn, the couple retired early and curled up under the warmth of a heavy quilted blanket.

In the middle of the night, the woman, Olivia, slipped from bed to use the bathroom. When she returned, she found the room freezing cold with its curtains dancing in the moonlit window. Her husband must have opened the window for some air without realizing how chilly it was outside, and then quickly fallen back asleep. How typical, she thought.

Olivia crossed the cold floor to the window, only to find it securely closed. Nor was there a draft that would explain either the numbing chill or the flowing curtains. Shivering from the cold and perhaps a touch of fear, for she was sure some ghostly entity was making its presence known, she crawled back into bed, seeking the warmth of the blankets and the comfort of her husband's presence.

Just as she was about to drift off, Olivia was pulled from her sleep by the pitiful sound of a young child crying. "It sounded like a little girl, so sad and lonely, and there was something about it that terrified me," she remembers. "But it was short and soft enough that I thought it might be my mind playing a trick."

Moments later, Olivia became aware that someone was in the hallway beyond the door. *Pad, pad, pad …* the soft cushioned sound of light feet walking down the carpeted corridor. The footsteps stopped for a moment outside her door. Olivia lay paralyzed by fright, eyes fixed on the door, praying that darkness would hide her from whatever lurked just beyond her room. She was sure that at any moment the knob would turn, the door would slowly swing open, and the deathly image of a long-dead child would stand framed in her doorway.

Then, *pad, pad, pad …* down the hallway it went, and she heard the soft passage as the unseen person descended the staircase. Had she not been afraid to breathe, Olivia would have screamed with relief. "I had trouble sleeping after that," she explains. "I felt such sympathy for this child — her crying just seemed to pull at my heart — but I was so scared. Looking back, I wonder if maybe she was looking for help that night, and I can't help thinking that I turned my back on her."

In the morning, Olivia's husband assured her there was some explanation besides the supernatural. But none was forthcoming. The couple learned that there had been no other guests staying in the inn that night, and the crying was too close and distinct to have come from a neighbouring building. Of that, Olivia is sure. "I'm a sceptic," she explains. "But I do believe the ghost of a young child haunts the Severn River Inn."

You can't help but feel at home at the Severn River Inn, so much so that when your stay is over it's difficult to tear yourself away from its warmth. Perhaps the same applies for spirits as well? Maybe the ghosts simply don't want to check out?

## Inn at the Falls

Nobody doubts the close relationship between a mother and her child. Their bond is eternal, spanning life and death. It's a connection that no one can accurately describe or understand. This bond seems to be at work at the Inn at the Falls in Bracebridge, a place where in years past a young woman suffered the ultimate tragedy. It was here that Mrs. Kirk not only lost her own life, but that of her unborn child as well.

Little do guests at this warm and quaint inn realize that they will be sharing their accommodations with a distraught ghostly woman, who can't seem to let go of the place where she lost everything. She gazes out of second-storey windows

The Inn at the Falls

(usually those of Room 101 or 105), her face etched in sorrow, her melancholy seemingly out of place in such a warm and inviting resort. In light of her tragic story, however, her unrelenting suffering is understandable.

The inn was originally built back in 1876 and was the home of Judge William C. Mahaffy, the first district judge of Muskoka and arguably the most prominent man about town. For many years, his home was the centre of social, political, and economic life in Bracebridge. However, a few years after the judge's 1912 death, his family sold the property.

For a time after the Mahaffys left, their home stood

vacant and it fell into a state of ill repair. In the early 1930s, a well-to-do man from Toronto by the name of Kirk purchased the grand old building and began restoration. He moved his young family in, and at first everyone was overjoyed with their new surroundings. The two young girls loved playing in the tower, perhaps imagining themselves to be damsels in distress awaiting salvation at the hands of a handsome prince, while their mother was taken by the charming architecture and the tranquility of its riverside setting. Although Mrs. Kirk was happy, her life did not feel complete. She desperately wanted a son. It was the one thing missing from her otherwise perfect family.

Mrs. Kirk's silent prayers seemed to be answered when she received the joyous news that she was with child again. Intuitively, she knew it was a boy, and was elated. As the months passed and her pregnancy began to show, Mrs. Kirk grew ever happier. She glowed with the radiance reserved for expecting mothers, and she savoured every moment of her pregnancy, for she knew it was a blessing.

One night, as her term was nearing completion, Mrs. Kirk became restless in bed. Rather than keep her husband up with her tossing and turning, she decided to walk about the house until the baby inside her settled. She gave her husband a light kiss and then slipped from the room. No one knows how it happened — perhaps she suffered from a premature contraction — but Mrs. Kirk fell as she was going down the stairs. The sickening thud of her crumpling to the floor awoke her husband, but by the time he arrived she was already dead. So, too, was her unborn child.

Though death may have taken Mrs. Kirk, it did not pull her away from the Inn at the Falls. Her presence is often announced by strange phenomenon, such as showers unexpectedly turning on and off on their own accord or the sudden random flipping of television channels. In 1995, noted U.S. psychic, Geraldine Page, visited the inn and noted several ghosts in residence, including a woman, who "was moving back and forth in the hallway, seemingly concerned for an unborn child." This surely must have been Mrs. Kirk.

You often hear noises in the night, especially in older buildings where the creaks of floorboards under foot and the groans of settling timbers can be mistaken for the unearthly cries of an apparition. But for one pregnant guest staying in Room 106 at the inn, it was not an easily explainable noise she heard late one evening. The pacing of a pregnant woman, up and down the second-floor hallway, awakened the woman. The guest in Room 106 could not help but overhear the conversation of a husband consoling his wife about the child she was carrying. Like many expectant first-time mothers, the inn's latest guest was frightened and apprehensive, afraid of the unknown. Feeling like she was eavesdropping, she tried not to listen.

The next morning, bothered by what she had heard the night before, she couldn't help but ask the management how the other pregnant woman was doing. The guest hoped that

A trip down the stairs at Inn at the Falls ended the lives of a
woman and her unborn child, and gave birth to a tragic legend.

the pregnant woman's worries had been soothed away by the
care her husband had shown. To her surprise, she was told
that there were no other guests staying in the inn that night.
She was confused. She knew what she had heard, and certainly the compassion she felt for the pregnant woman was
real enough.

Today, the Inn at the Falls attracts all kinds of guests: ones
who want a romantic getaway or a businessperson stopping

for the night. Some come specifically because of the ghosts. It so happened that two elderly sisters, after hearing of the odd happenings at the inn, were compelled to visit and set the record straight. These women, who turned out to be the daughters of Mr. Kirk, were extremely sceptical of the ghost stories. Arriving at the inn, they were swept away with childhood memories. Neither one could understand why anyone would believe that their former home was haunted. Certainly they had never experienced anything out of the ordinary during their years there. After reminiscing about the childhood they had spent at the inn, the Kirk sisters approached a staff member to ask about the ghosts. They were told that many people, staff and guests alike, had seen and felt the presence of a young woman with child. It was also explained that local lore suggested that the ghost was that of a woman who fell down the stairs when she was near to term, killing both herself and her unborn child.

Bent on setting things straight, the Kirk sisters were shocked at what they were hearing. The story they were listening to bore uncanny resemblance to a little-known part of their family history. The Kirk sisters had known for years that their father had another wife prior to marrying their mother. The first wife had suffered an unfortunate accident in this very building. Could it be that the stories were true, that the first Mrs. Kirk had fallen down the staircase and died, along with her unborn child? Could the ghost wandering the halls of the Inn at the Falls be the spirit of their father's first wife?

The circumstances seemed too similar to be a coincidence. The Kirk sisters — sceptics when they arrived — left the inn as believers.

Perhaps more disturbing was the experience of a young married couple who stayed at the inn for a brief holiday a few years back. The wife, who identified herself as Stephanie, was a few months pregnant at the time and the trip to Bracebridge was intended as a respite before the hectic sleepless existence of new motherhood was cast upon her. She found her stay perfectly soothing. Her husband, Paul, had a slightly different experience.

It started on their first evening there. The shower had turned on by itself, which was perplexing but not exactly unsettling. Paul slipped out of bed to turn it off. When he returned, he swore that he saw a dark-haired lady staring intently at his sleeping wife from across the room. Then, in the blink of an eye, she was gone. Paul saw this woman several times during the stay, always watching his wife, always in their bedroom, always disappearing as soon as he noticed her.

Upon reflection, he believes the ghost wore an old-fashioned dress that ballooned around the waist and that she might have been pregnant herself. He also remembers the intensity of the ghost's gaze, and the sadness etched in her pale face. What disturbs him the most was that he could never decide whether the spirit was standing watch over Stephanie to protect her and her unborn child, or whether she was jealous that his wife would have the child that the ghostly one was denied. Happily, Stephanie and Paul did indeed bear a son five months later.

Though there are other ghosts in residence at the Inn at the Falls, it is Mrs. Kirk who seems to touch guests most profoundly. She continues to haunt the second floor, replaying the final moments before the accident stole her life and snatched away her dreams. Mrs. Kirk walks the halls as she did 70 years ago during those nights when the child growing inside her was too active to allow her to sleep. Back then, her midnight walks were moments of pure happiness. Today, they are torturous reminders of her great loss, the child she so desperately wanted but which fate denied her.

Ultimately, though, this is not really a story of loss, but a story of profound love, one that endures beyond death. The kind of love only a mother feels, even for a child not yet born.

# *Chapter 3*
# Mysterious Places

There is something mysterious about Native American legends that captivates us all. From ancient burial grounds to sacred sites, the spirit world is part of the everyday life of many Native people. Their pride, their rich culture, and even their fears echo through these enchanted places, begging us to investigate their secrets.

### The Thornbury Mound

The awe-inspiring wonder known as the Thornbury Mound broods over the Beaver Valley that stretches out below it, casting a mysterious shadow that even modern science hasn't been able to shed light upon. It has perplexed us for two centuries, and despite decades of serious study, we're no closer today to unwrapping the secrets of the mound than we were when it was first happened upon in the early nineteenth century.

The Thornbury Mound is among the most unique sights one is liable to find anywhere in Ontario. It's an ancient, possibly prehistoric, man-made monument located on a hill above the small Georgian Bay town of Thornbury. Perfectly symmetrical and made of red clay, the mound stands some 10 metres high and 80 metres long, and is topped by a boulder with a line of crystal pointing due north. It's clearly not a natural formation, but no one is quite sure what to make of it. The mound's origins and purpose are lost in a swirling fog of folklore and speculation, denser than any mist that might blow in off nearby Georgian Bay.

Europeans have known of the existence of the Thornbury Mound since 1836, and it is referred to locally as the Indian Burial Ground. The Native peoples who originally inhabited the region were the Wyandot. This cultured and sophisticated people lived in large palisade villages and developed complex agricultural methods. Many believe that the Wyandot or their forebears erected the mound. They point to the other native burial mounds that dot Ontario as evidence to support this supposition. However, the theory is somewhat marred by the fact that none of the other mounds located across the province are as large or as impressive as Thornbury.

Thornbury's mound is one of seven similar mounds found along the Niagara Escarpment. The others are located near Blue Mountain, Creemore, the Hockley Valley, and the forks of the Credit River. They all seem to follow river routes into the interior that may once have been part of an ancient trading route. Natives extracted copper from Isle Royale on Lake Superior as early as 3000 years ago, and jewellery made from Lake Superior ore has been discovered as far south as Alabama and Florida. Clearly, this was a complex and sophisticated trade network.

Some archeologists believe that the Thornbury Mound was a vital cog in these early trading routes, and not a burial mound at all. They believe that the mound may have been a point of reference for traders travelling from as far away as the southern United States. They suggest that the boulder on its peak may have served as a signpost or a navigational aid, as the view from the top of the mound extends beyond the Beaver Valley to the next mound in the chain, which is located at Blue Mountain.

Other experts have more radical opinions. A few have drawn comparisons to Celtic burial mounds in the British Isles, such as the 5000-year-old mound at Newgrange, Ireland. This mound is eerily similar to Thornbury in dimension and shape. The experts point to the findings of their ground-probing radar, which have detected electrical anomalies identical to those of sites in Europe, as proof of the mound's true origin and nature. The theory is that ancient Celts travelled across the Atlantic between the years 500 B.C.E. and 1500 C.E., sailing down the St. Lawrence and into the Great Lakes system in search of copper deposits. When they arrived, they built the mound either as a signpost for their vessels or as a burial mound for a great leader or, perhaps, both. The theory seems far-fetched on the surface, but the Celts were accomplished sailors and stone carvings found in Newfoundland resembling Celtic script suggest that it is possible that these early European people may have crossed the Atlantic.

There are yet other names bandied about as the creators of the mound. Could they be, for example, Irish monks, Viking settlers from Greenland, or even a hypothetical group of Scots known as the Albans?

Beyond being of unknown origin, the mound holds other secrets as well. Strange lights have been seen, and photographed, emanating from its peak. Further, local tradition holds that it is the source of great spiritual power for Native peoples. Some believe that the energy associated with the mound heals the body and cures disease and that it was, and possibly still is, important in vision quests. If this location does indeed hold special properties, it might explain why the mound was originally built. Could it have been a site of spiritual or ceremonial celebrations? Those who hold to this belief, including Robert Burcher, an amateur archeologist who has studied the monument for almost a decade, have named the site Shaman's Mound.

As is common with mysterious and mystical sites the world over, the Thornbury Mound is home to numerous unusual happenings. A spectral Native has on occasion been seen atop the mound. The figure is present only for a few fleeting seconds — two or three exhilarating heartbeats at most — before he vanishes right before the eyes of astonished observers. The spectre has been reported to fade into the earth as if entering the tomb that folklore suggests is buried below the mound. The experience leaves people rubbing their eyes and squinting into the hazy gloom. Interestingly, the spirit is seen most frequently at dusk (although it has also been seen at dawn). This corresponds to the time of day in which the unexplained glow is also reported to occur. Eerie, ethereal sounds have also been heard ... perhaps the melancholy chanting of an ancient native ceremony.

Several years back an unearthly experience occurred and was witnessed by a small group of college students. It was the kind of gloomy mid-winter day that Georgian Bay is known for. The dawn brought very little illumination to the landscape. Everything was covered in a damp grey mist. Skeletal trees poked through the snow like zombies clawing out from their graves, while evergreens bowed under the weight of their cloaks of white. Here and there, the snow-laden tips of farmers' fence posts appeared above the drifts. No glimmer of sunrise gave even a hint as to what direction the students were travelling in.

The brilliant glow emanating from the mound caught the attention of the group. The glow could easily have been mistaken for a brilliant sunrise — except for the complete absence of the sun on that grey morning. Intrigued, the youths bundled up against the weather and trekked off through the snow, intent on finding the source of the mysterious light. But, as they approached the mound, the light disappeared. It wasn't sudden, like a light switching off, but rather slow and gradual, as if one were dimming an oil lamp. Reaching the top of the mound, they found nothing to indicate any possible source of the light. The sun was still obscured by clouds; there were no ashes to mark a fire, and no footprints to suggest that anyone else had been there since the snow began.

But something *was* there. A swirling mist, a kind of whitish fog, enveloped one of the students. It was cold, so cold that she felt it right through her winter garments, and she later claimed that, while embraced by the mysterious mist, she had heard faint whispers. She couldn't make out the words — but the message was clear — the spirit was angry.

Why this spirit, presumably that of an ancient holy man, continues to linger long after death is a question that remains unanswered, one of the many linked to Thornbury Mound.

We may never know who made the mound, or indeed, why. Its origins lost to us, the mound remains mysterious and melancholy, especially so with the cold stark Georgian Bay serving as a backdrop. The Thornbury Mound stands as a silent testimony to an earlier people, whose skills and beliefs we can only marvel at thousands of years after they laboured to produce this mysterious monument.

## Ekarenniondi

A mysterious rock formation, known as Worshipping Rock or *Ekarenniondi* (which means "where the rock stands out" in the Huron tongue) is the highlight of the Scenic Caves Nature Preserve near Collingwood, Ontario. It is a stunning and atmospheric monument, proof that the timeless forces of nature often create landscapes more impressive than any that the human mind can conceive. Its unique majesty, its rugged beauty, and the tranquillity of its surroundings make the setting almost magical, and it's easy to see why Native people revere Ekarenniondi.

The rock is far more than a photographer's dream, however. Ekarenniondi is also the home of Leuantido, the apparition of a beautiful Huron maiden and her ghostly lover. They have continued their doomed romance for more than five centuries now, and the courting shows no sign of letting up.

Traditional Huron people avoid the area around Ekarenniondi from sunset to sunrise because the rock, as magnificent as it is, is also the centrepiece of their haunting story of eternal love. It began innocently enough, when a chief from the Erie tribe, whose name is lost to human memory, came to the shores of Georgian Bay to trade amongst the Huron. What he found, however, was far more valuable than any trade item. He became mesmerized by the breathtaking beauty of a young Huron maiden.

As the daughter of a prominent Huron chief, the beautiful Leuantido was destined to marry a mighty warrior in an

Hauntingly beautiful, or simply haunted? Collingwood
Caves are a place where history and mystery entwine.

alliance that would enhance her tribe's status. In the mean-
time, she was expected to remain faithful to her tribe and
utterly obedient to her father's wishes. But when she met the
dashing Erie chief, she could not help but fall in love with
him. Leuantido instinctively flung off the constraints of her
position, and revelled in the excitement of a forbidden courtship. The lovers' romance blossomed as the weeks passed,

and their hopes for a life together resulted in a passionate recklessness. They became fearful, knowing that their relationship was taboo.

Leuantido's beloved had approached the Huron chief to ask for permission to court his daughter. It must have taken great courage to do so, for Leuantido's father was an intimidating man known for his volatile temper. Not surprisingly, the chief angrily refused to sanction the relationship, and threatened the young suitor with death should he ignore the decision.

No threat could deter the young lovers. Passion blinded them to the danger they courted by continuing their furtive encounters. As weeks turned into months, the affair continued unabated. Eventually, however, Leuantido's brothers found out about the illicit moonlight meetings. Enraged, the brothers decided to take matters into their own hands and end the relationship. Could Leuantido's father have played a role in their decision? The brothers followed the lovers one night and ambushed the impassioned Erie chief. They fell upon him with a vengeance and by the time their anger was sated, their tomahawks were stained red with blood. Leuantido's beloved lay motionless at their feet.

Leuantido witnessed the entire attack and, screaming hysterically, had begged her brothers to show mercy. But she knew they would not stop. She watched helplessly as her siblings picked up her lover's limp and bloodied body and callously threw him off the cliff. His name was upon her lips as his body smashed against the rocks below. Her heart had gone over the cliff with him, and was broken in bits, just as brutally as was her lover's body.

Leuantido's punishment for disobeying her father's wishes was less severe than that handed out by her enraged brothers. Nevertheless, she was never the same again. The trauma of seeing her loved one slaughtered at the hands of her siblings caused something to snap in the young woman's mind. Weeks passed, and with each day Leuantido became more and more despondent. She knew she could not live without her beloved. Finally, in desperation late one moonlit night, she stumbled to the scene of his demise — and after agonizing over the events that had led to her lover's death — Leuantido pitched herself over the brink to be by his side forever. Her brothers found her shattered body upon the rocks.

Despite being together for all eternity, the violent nature of their deaths made the couple restless. Their spirits still wander the scene of their tragic affair and, under the cover of darkness; they repeatedly replay their forbidden rendezvous. Many Huron have subsequently stumbled upon their ghostly meetings, and those who did felt an overwhelming sense of despair for the lovers doomed by their unsanctioned love. Legend says that their unearthly presence has stained the area, cursing it for all time. As a result, it has long been avoided by Native peoples.

Today, Ekarenniondi is marvelled at by thousands of tourists every year. The nature preserve closes well before dark. Could this be to allow Leuantido and her beloved the uninterrupted intimacy they craved in life? No doubt, the spirits of the lovers continue to haunt the area. Sometimes they are actually seen. Other times, Leuantido's voice drifts over the rocky landscape, mournfully calling out for her lover.

## The Island of the Giant's Tomb

Giant's Tomb Island, in Georgian Bay near Penetanguishene, is said to be home to foul creatures eager to claim mortal lives. Combined with the sudden storms, hidden shoals, and unpredictable currents typical of the surrounding waters, these creatures make maritime travel in the area a dangerous task. Even seasoned boaters are cautious near Giant's Tomb, and have been as far back in history as written records reach.

The powerful image of Giant's Tomb left a haunting impression on the Huron who are native to the area. When Jesuit missionaries arrived in the 1600s, they recorded how the Huron shunned the island as cursed, or worse, as haunted. Even the bravest warrior and the most skilled canoe handler refused to venture near. That's why, even though Giant's Tomb is a large island around 405 hectares in size, no native archeological sites have ever been found. Something, or some things, kept the Huron at bay.

One belief is that Giant's Tomb was inhabited by the "ant-gaunt," an evil water serpent that fed on the corpses of those who drowned. According to native lore, the ant-gaunt lived in a cave beneath Giant's Tomb and was responsible for conjuring mighty storms. This belief was cemented by the volatile nature of the portion of Georgian Bay where Giant's Tomb is located. Known as The Gap by locals, the water here is 70 metres deep and forms a confluence that results in the occurrence of storms that seem to come out of the blue. The water is known to blow up very quickly, creating metre-and-a-half waves that can easily swamp a canoe.

The Huron often called upon the ant-gaunt in hopes that the creature would quell its wrath and calm the violent waters. But even if these entreaties were successful and the waters remained placid, travellers knew that, beneath the surface, the massive sea monster was keeping pace with their canoes — quietly waiting for the opportunity to strike. If a canoe overturned, the only way an individual could ensure his own survival was to force his companions below the waves, sacrificing them to the ever hungry ant-gaunt in exchange for his own life. It was the ultimate deal with the devil, and it seems the creature took perverse pleasure in watching humans turn upon one another.

Aside from the ant-gaunt, however, there were other reasons to avoid the island. In ancient times, the mighty god Ki-chi-ki-wa-na resided on the southern shores of Georgian Bay, living among his people. He was a being of immense proportions. His headdress was made from the feathers of thousands of birds, the robes he wore around his torso comprised 600 beaver pelts, and the necklace that hung from his neck was made from dozens of tree stumps.

Everything about Ki-chi-ki-wa-na was imposing, including his temperament. The local Native peoples loved having him as an ally because he was a formidable warrior, but they also feared his temper and his fits of violent anger. His people believed that all Ki-chi-ki-wa-na needed to settle him down was the love of a good woman, and so the Native peoples, in an effort to appease their tantrum-prone god, began to display their most beautiful and even-tempered women, in the hope that he would soon select a bride.

The god selected Wanika, the most beautiful maid of them all. But she was strong-willed and had a mind of her own. She rejected his offer, as her heart had already been given to a warrior from her tribe, and she was determined to marry him. To escape her giant-sized suitor, Wanika fled to the north.

Ki-chi-ki-wa-na was predictably upset. He flew into a rage, the likes of which had never been seen. In his tantrum, he repeatedly scooped up handfuls of rocks and earth, and threw them into Georgian Bay after the fleeing maiden. In so doing, he created the five bays on the southern shore of Georgian Bay, which he gouged out of the land by his massive fingers, into 30,000 islands. When he grew tired and his anger subsided, Ki-chi-ki-wa-na lay down at the base of the islands he had created and fell into an eternal sleep. Sediment formed over his prone body, creating the island of the Giant's Tomb.

Legend says the island should be avoided, particularly

at night or in the fall and winter when Ki-chi-ki-wa-na's sleep grows fitful and causes the seasonal storms that sweep across the bay. Those that fail to heed this warning may disturb the giant's sleep and thereby face the direst of consequences. Evil spirits, the past victims of Ki-chi-ki-wa-na's anger, haunt the island and prey upon the unwary.

By the nineteenth century, the settlers of Simcoe County and the mariners who plied Georgian Bay also feared Giant's Tomb. It was an even more superstitious time, and the native legends resonated with those of the immigrants. This was particularly true of Giant's Tomb because Ki-chi-ki-wa-na symbolizes the destructive force of nature, something the early settlers, especially the sailors of Lake Huron, had became all too acquainted with.

A few old tales suggest that, among the early Europeans, Giant's Tomb earned a reputation as a cursed island, a land-scape haunted by ghostly lights that would lure ships to their doom. And indeed many wrecks, dating back to the early part of the twentieth century and some perhaps before, litter the rocks along this stretch of Georgian Bay.

During stormy weather, a distinct and uneasy chill ripples across the island's surface. And when the island is shrouded in darkness wind whispers through the trees, eerily suggesting movement where, perhaps, none exists. Some claim to have seen apparitions on the island. Few people visit Giant's Tomb, and fewer still have willingly spent the night.

In September of 1922, Jim Parr, a Native from Parry

Sound, spent a terror-filled night on the island, but he definitely had no say in the matter. In fact, he was lucky to be alive. The fury of Ki-chi-ki-wa-na nearly claimed him, his father, and another fisherman as its latest victims. At the time, Jim was barely more than a boy, and the maritime excursion seemed like an exciting adventure. The three men set sail from Parry Sound for Penetanguishene with nearly a ton of fish in their 24-foot Collingwood skiff. All was well at first, but as the boat approached Giant's Tomb a cold front suddenly emerged, driving a foaming white sea ahead of it. The maelstrom bore down on the little schooner with unbridled ferocity. All the fishermen could do was race for the nearest shore 40 kilometres away, and hope that they could stay ahead of the storm's full fury.

Night fell. Angry lances of lightning punctuated the blackness. A ferocious gust of wind shredded the sail and splintered the mast, leaving the men at the mercy of the storm. A flash of lightning lit up the horizon, revealing the ominous shape of Giant's Tomb looming right ahead. Suddenly an enormous wave picked the craft up and threw it onto a shoal just off the island's shores — ripping a gaping hole in its hull. The skiff was grounded and rapidly taking on water, and though the safety of dry land was tantalizingly close at hand, no one dared to risk wading ashore in the heaving waters.

The three men spent miserable hours in the tiny cabin, shivering from the knee-deep water and surrounded by the night's impenetrable shroud of darkness. During the long wait for dawn, they heard rescuers walking across the deck. The footsteps resounded on the wooden boards, then stopped just short of the cabin. They were saved!

The men stepped out into the rain. There was no one there. This happened several times during the night, each time the men were certain they heard men on the deck. But there never were any rescuers at hand, nor could there be. The storm was too intense for any sane person to chance coming to their aid, even if would-be rescuers had known their location, which of course they didn't. Gradually, the superstitious fishermen realized that it was more likely that Ki-chi-ki-wa-na's fury had driven the boat ashore. They were sure that the angry giant was intent on sending the corpses of earlier victims aboard — to add three more wet graves to his tally.

How many lives has Giant's Tomb claimed over the centuries? Like so much about the island, the number of demised is wrapped in mystery and legend. What's known for sure is that for centuries, the Huron, the Ojibway, the Europeans, and many others have avoided Giant's Tomb and gazed on its majesty only from afar — and if legend is to be believed — for good reason.

Does the angry spirit surrounded by mist still inhabit Thornbury Mound? Do the lovers of Ekarenniondi continue their ghostly courtship? Does the ant-gaunt wait patiently for its next meal beneath the waves near Giant's Tomb? Is it possible that Ki-chi-ki-wa-na still sleeps restlessly under tons of rock, listening for intruders? Every time the waves cap white and a storm threatens along Georgian Bay, one must question whether they still exist ... just waiting.

## Chapter 4
# Murder Most Foul

hough we in Canada often tend to over-
look our past, our nation, and Ontario in
particular, has a rich and varied history full
of drama, passion, heartbreak, and violence. These elements
have over time produced a multitude of ghosts and spectres
that make for fascinating and exciting stories. If even a frac-
tion of the tales are based on fact versus fiction then Ontario
is, and will remain, alive with the restless spirits who relive
the past in their wanderings through the present.

**The Headless Peddler**
We often hear the phrase, "Don't lose your head." It's an
expression, of course, and we don't mean it literally, or do we?
For one lonely traveller — who had the misfortune to wander

into a biased, backroads community in central Ontario in the 1890s — that was exactly his fate.

The lead story in the *Dufferin Advertiser* on February 25, 1892, gave a lurid account of the grisly murder and decapitation of a peddler in the village of Loretto. This bloodshed was just the latest in a string of violent crimes that had cast a dark pall over Adjala Township. Thus, in the latter half of the nineteenth century, Loretto acquired something of a ghoulish reputation. Its rolling hills were stained red with blood, a stage for real-life murders and betrayals that would make Shakespeare envious.

A tiny farming community located 12 kilometres from Tottenham, Loretto was never much more than an inn, a store, and a few scattered homes. Yet its strategic location at a busy crossroads ensured a steady trade for the tavern run by Mrs. Gamble. It was this tavern, or more specifically the spirits that flowed within it, that was to blame for much of the trouble. Alcohol, mixed with a healthy dose of religious intolerance, pitted the majority Irish Catholics of the region against the scattered Protestants (Orangemen), creating a raucous brew.

For most of the century, and continuing on into the early decades of the twentieth century, the "wilds of Adjala" were considered akin to the American West. It was a rowdy place with little respect for justice — save that which was handed out with club or a meaty fist.

"The surrounding country is given up for farming,"

noted the *Dufferin Advertiser*, "but a number of undesirable characters infest the section. Law is an unknown quantity to many of the latter, and might is right with them. Rows and brutal assaults are not uncommon, and murders have been committed in the locality on several occasions."

In the late 1880s, for example, a bailiff was beheaded with an axe in the vicinity of Loretto, and a local jury acquitted the guilty party. Earlier, in the 1860s, "Orange" John Irwin was attacked and murdered in the woods during election time. A decade before that, a Protestant trader known as the "Orange" Peddler was presumed murdered in the swamps near Loretto. Only his pack and some personal belongings were found.

The tightly knit community was wary of outsiders. Closing ranks to protect their own allowed many guilty parties to escape penalties for their wrongdoings. Oddly, there never seemed to be any eyewitnesses. Local officials and local juries were notoriously biased or, in some cases, intimidated into impotence. Investigations into injustices were almost always stonewalled by the stubborn silence of the settlers.

This all makes the events of January 25, 1892, hard to unravel. On this fateful evening, an inspector of weights and measures, Mr. Lyon, happened to find himself in Loretto. Faced with bitter cold and rapidly encroaching darkness, he sought solace in Gamble's Inn. Among the other patrons that night were a humble peddler and a crowd of village loafers. Drinks flowed fast that evening as the men sought to warm themselves with alcohol. Soon the locals, heavily inebriated, began singing boisterous tunes. Lyon watched the locals from across the room, as they demanded that the peddler participate in their merriment. Knowing the drunkards were Catholics, the peddler warily declined, as the only songs he knew were Orange songs. The men insisted, however, threatening the by-now thoroughly frightened peddler with punishment if he didn't comply. Reluctantly, the weary traveller acquiesced.

It was about this time that Lyon, who had been observing the unfolding drama all along, excused himself and went to bed. Shortly thereafter, he heard the peddler withdraw to his upstairs room as well, closely followed by the gang of increasingly hostile drunks. Enraged by some perceived slight, or perhaps merely by the peddler's religious affiliation, the drunks forced their way into the peddler's chamber. According to Lyon, "The brawl became worse in the peddler's room, and it was quite evident that the poor man was being roughly handled. Curses and oaths broke the stillness of the night, and the peddler could be heard uttering hoarse appeals for mercy."

Suddenly, everything went eerily silent. Lyon, who had barricaded himself in his own room as soon as the commotion started, was sure something terrible had befallen the peddler. But, afraid for his own safety, he warily awaited morning.

When at last Lyon emerged from behind his secured

door, he found the floor and the hall leading downstairs stained with blood. Descending the stairs, his stomach was assaulted by a horrible stench that clung to the barroom. Still following the trail of blood, Lyon made his way over to the wood stove, where he paused. Mustering up the courage, he moved aside the lid. Inside the stove, "baking on the coals, lay the charred remains of the peddler." Horrified, he realized there was one part missing — the head.

Repulsed and terrified, he quickly packed his bags and put the horrid scene behind him. Eventually, word of what Lyon had seen leaked out, creating a sensational story. The *Toronto Mail* even sent a reporter to investigate, but as always, the reporter found few locals who were willing to talk about the incident. The *Dufferin Advertiser* concluded that fear suppressed the truth: "Religious feeling runs high in Adjala and the man who had too much to say when Roman Catholicism was implicated might get his head broken on some future occasion for his pains."

No official investigation was ever launched to determine the truth behind the story, and the grisly events of that night were rarely spoken of again. But, despite everyone's best efforts, they will never be forgotten. How can they be when the peddler himself, headless and despondent, periodically appears to refresh fading memories of Loretto's bloody past? It seems he refuses to go gently into eternity or to allow the community to ease their guilty consciences. He isn't just looking for justice. He is also looking for his missing head.

Could the murderous thugs have taken it as a grim memento of their deeds? Perhaps.

In the years since his death, the headless peddler has been seen numerous times wandering along the isolated stretches of country roads that surround Loretto. When people are comfortably settled into their warm beds, the ghost aimlessly wanders through the night, startling those few souls courageous or foolish enough to brave the darkness and the ruffians that lurk within it. He always appears suddenly in the gloom, as if materializing out of the darkness itself, wearing simple clothes and carrying a pack upon his back. The peddler is reported to look real enough, if not for the gaping void where his head should be.

An elderly farmer returning from his fields spotted him one night. It was the 1930s, the height of the Great Depression, and the old man thought the figure walking slowly down the country lane to be another out-of-work man in search of employment. He pulled up his team and hollered a hello. The kind man was intent on offering to put the stranger up for the night in his barn to keep him out of the autumn chill. When no response was forthcoming, he tried to hail him once more. Again, no response. At this point, the silent traveller was just approaching the horses, and the farmer realized why the man had not acknowledged his greetings. He had no head. Then, slowly, the figure faded into nothingness — leaving the farmer alone — gripped with intangible fear.

The elderly man raced home as fast as his old horses

would carry him. Even when he was safe within the warm confines of his house and with a blazing fire roaring in the hearth, it was hours before the unnatural chill that blanketed him lifted. From that day forward, the farmer took pains to ensure that he left his fields well before sundown, leaving even earlier if he had to pass along the stretch of road frequented by the headless stranger.

While the spectral peddler is only seen along deserted roads, he may, in the past, have sought the warmth of Gamble's Inn on particularly cold nights. When the winds blew harsh and strong and temperatures dipped to uncomfortable levels, the ghost's restless presence was often felt in the tavern's bar. Perhaps the ghost was attracted to the spot where he was brutally slain and his head removed. Unnatural cold spots chilled patrons. Scratching sounds, like fingernails desperately clawing at wood, were heard on the floorboards — and there was an inexplicable waft of warm air that smelled of smoke — and of something far worse. It was enough to unsettle even the hardest of men.

The ravages of time and the elements have since taken the bloodstained Gamble's Inn, leaving the lonely and forgotten ghostly peddler to wander aimlessly. And as long as he continues to prowl the quiet roads around the village, the past can never be left behind. Sightings of the spectre serve as a grim reminder that justice will never be his. Could you remain calm in his deathly presence or — as the spectre once did — would you lose your head?

**Together in Life — Apart in Death**

Is love, as they say, eternal? Does it extend beyond the grave? Can it survive even without a physical host to inhabit? These are questions countless numbers of people have asked over the millennium. Perhaps it is our attempt to come to grips with our own mortality or perhaps it is to help us understand the meaning of life. These questions have particular relevance for many who are acquainted with a certain graveyard in Ontario, the Richmond Hill Presbyterian Church Cemetery. And they have another question to add to the debate. Do tragic lovers forever haunt graveyards, their souls trapped in our world by a combination of undying passion and the brutal nature of their deaths?

Today, Richmond Hill is a burgeoning city just north of Toronto. In the early nineteenth century it was a quiet rural farming community in which little of consequence occurred. The hardworking citizens went about their lives with nary a noteworthy event to break the monotony of their existence. And that, by and large, is how they liked it.

But things changed suddenly in 1843 when the name Richmond Hill screamed from the front pages of newspapers across all of Upper Canada (as Ontario was then known) and across the entire nation. The little village had played host to what was then regarded as the province's most notorious murder case.

Thomas Kinnear resided just over a kilometre and a half north of Richmond Hill in a fine home on a sprawling farm.

The young man didn't fit in with the rest of the community, however. He was described as a gentleman farmer "of considerable means" who lived a life of "careless ease and self-indulgence." One of his principle indulgences involved members of the fairer sex. It seems Kinnear was something of a playboy. Indeed, it's likely that Kinnear had been sent to Upper Canada and given a sizable stipend upon which to live by a father embarrassed by his son's flighty ways. Rumour has it that he had been involved in a scandal, probably an ill-advised romantic dalliance with a married woman back in his native England, and was exiled to avoid the firestorm of controversy.

It wasn't long before the young gentleman of easy circumstance became the centre of whispered innuendo in his new home as well. But Kinnear's life changed when he hired the incredibly beautiful Nancy Montgomery as his live-in housekeeper. Their relationship was based on love as well as passion. And it soon became common knowledge that they were not only intimate but also deeply attached to each another. In the Victorian era, this was a major scandal, and Kinnear and Montgomery became pariahs in the community.

Unfortunately for the lovers, James McDermott, a 20-year-old Irish lad and Grace Marks, an Irish lassie who was all of 16, entered the picture. They were hired, individually, as household servants. James was a fairly nondescript young man, though it was suggested by some that he was a British army deserter. Grace, on the other hand, was anything but your average timid servant. She was, in fact, a stunning girl who had a way of using her charms to get what she wanted. Grace also had something of an Irish temper that came to the fore when she couldn't have that which she desired.

She desired Thomas Kinnear, but to her surprise she was rebuked. And that made her angry. Humiliated and incensed, Grace recruited James in a plot to kill Nancy Montgomery and Thomas Kinnear. She promised to marry him if only he did this one little favour for her. Smitten with Grace and resentful of his employer's comfortable life and easy supply of cash, the lad was only too happy to oblige. They married, but little did he know that "till death do us part" would come less than a year later.

James and Grace had only been in the Kinnear employ for three weeks when, on July 18, 1843, both Thomas and Nancy were brutally slain. Nancy was killed first, strangled slowly by James. Some reports claim she was also cut up with an axe, her body hidden under a washtub in the basement. Kinnear was next. Upon returning home from a trip to York (now Toronto), he was ambushed and shot dead through the heart. James and Grace rifled his pockets for money, ransacked the home for valuables, and then saddled a horse and fled the gruesome scene. The desperate pair attempted to make for the safety of the U.S. border, but at 5 a.m. the next day Mr. Kingswell, the high bailiff, arrested them at Lewiston. They had come within a breath of succeeding with their plan.

James McDermott was sentenced to hang. To his dying breath he stuck to the story that Grace was behind the double murder. For her part, Grace Marks was also found guilty, but no one knew exactly what do with her. Was she insane, a helpless victim, or was she the mastermind behind the murders, as most now believe? The verdict was complicated because of her youth and attractive looks.

In the end, she was sentenced to life imprisonment in Kingston Penitentiary, but spent most of her time shuttling back and forth between prison and an insane asylum. After many petitions pleading her case, Grace Marks was released and given a pardon. She moved to New York, changed her name and, apparently, married once again.

As for the victims, in death as in life they were stigmatized by their unseemly affair. They are buried in the southwest corner of Richmond Hill Presbyterian Cemetery, a considerable distance from the community's more reputable citizens. Nancy's body lies at Thomas' feet, in the only grave in the cemetery that lies along a north-south line.

Some suggest the grisly nature of their demise and perhaps the insulting manner in which they were buried has conspired to prevent Kinnear and Montgomery from resting in peace. Their ghosts apparently haunt the cemetery to this day.

One teenage girl who visited the cemetery late at night had a ghostly experience. "I heard someone or something breathing behind me, right behind my ear," she wrote via e-mail. "It sounded like the person was having trouble breathing. But when I turned around there was no one there. I ran away and later told my friends, but they thought I was just imagining it." Did this young girl hear Kinnear's last breaths, right after he exclaimed, "Oh my God, I'm shot!" Or was it perhaps Nancy Montgomery struggling for air as James squeezed the life from her?

Over the past 160 years there have been several similar reports. One account, however, is quite unnerving. While playing in the cemetery, two young boys heard something that sounded like a wooden door suddenly and violently swinging open. This loud noise, followed by a ghastly choking sound, was so chilling to the lads that they fled with haste. According to folklore, the date was the anniversary of McDermott's execution. Many believe the lads had heard the spectral replaying of the murderer's last moments — the sounds of the gallows trapdoor dropping open — and McDermott's life slipping away.

There are even stories of people seeing the ghostly lovers themselves, either individually or together hand in hand, solemnly walking the cemetery grounds. It seems that despite being vilified for his relationship with Nancy Montgomery in life, Thomas Kinnear continues to keep company with her in death. Such was the depth of his love for her.

The tale of Kinnear and Montgomery's affair and the gruesome story of their untimely death have largely been forgotten today. It seems, however, that the victims themselves cannot forget; it's as if they are unwilling to be entirely relegated to the annals of history. The lovers refuse to depart from the community that treated them with such disdain in life.

Perhaps their spirits simply seek vindication and will quietly fade away if only they are laid to rest in a more acceptable fashion. Clearly, being isolated from others in the graveyard, with Nancy lying horizontally at Thomas's feet, is humiliating. It might behoove the community to exhume the lovers and to bury them respectfully, side by side.

## The Ghost of the Queen's Hotel

Spectral yelling, the screams of a man in agonizing pain, and disembodied footsteps walking across the aging floorboards made the Queen's Hotel anything but welcoming. The ghost of a rumrunner who died a horrible death was said to haunt this notorious building.

The tragedy dates back to the 1920s. Prohibition was introduced in Ontario in 1916 and overnight, it became illegal to purchase or drink alcohol. Merely sitting down with a glass of wine at dinner or having a cold one after a long day at work meant breaking the law. The "noble experiment," as Prohibition was called, was intended to reduce crime and poverty. Instead, it heralded in more than a decade of greed, mayhem, and violence. Mobsters turned the sale of alcohol into multi-million dollar empires. And while most people associate mobsters, Tommy guns, and speakeasies with the United States, Canada had more than its share of all three.

One of the most notorious centres for such illicit activities in Ontario was the Queen's Hotel, located in Aurora, just north of Toronto. Most houses of ill repute lost their notoriety after Prohibition was lifted, but the same cannot be said of this establishment. Within its aging walls, in which one final event was a violent murder, the illegal booze-soaked dramas of the 1920s continued to play on in a shadowy echo that resonated for years afterwards.

At one time during the nineteenth century the Queen's Hotel was the most elegant hostelry in Aurora. In an era when most hotels were little more than taverns and way-stops for stagecoaches, the Queen's Hotel was notable for its refined hospitality. For nearly four decades after its 1865 founding, the hotel prospered.

By the turn of the century, however, the heyday of hotels in Aurora — and indeed of all small-town hotels across Ontario — was long past. Those that survived did so mostly as glorified taverns. At least ... until Prohibition was loosed upon Ontario in 1916. When the sale of alcohol became illegal, many hotels lost their sole remaining source of revenue. Few survived.

The Queen's Hotel was one of those that persevered, though it sold its soul to the devil to do so. As soon as Prohibition was implemented, speakeasies popped up all over North America to quench thirst and to provide the excitement that a war-weary nation was looking for. Otherwise law-abiding individuals, men and women, would come to throw back the whiskey and enjoy a night of revelry. The Queen's Hotel was one of dozens, if not hundreds, of speakeasies operating in Ontario.

By this time the inn was weathered and rapidly deteriorating. And, in keeping with its degraded appearance, the clientele tended to be less than savoury. The Queen's became a seedy establishment, frequented by individuals seeking the baser pleasures of life. Whiskey was sold for 50 cents a glass, serious gambling was commonplace, and bookies facilitated efforts to "run the numbers." There were even whispers that "ladies of the night" plied their immoral trade within.

Emotions ran high, no doubt fuelled by the "white lightning" being downed. More than one case of festering resentment boiled over into violence. This booze-driven mayhem may have set the scene for the haunting that plagued the hotel a few years later. Whatever its cause, a puzzling and senseless murder left a dark stain of blood and anguish ingrained in the very wood of the old hotel.

While it's certainly possible the murder was the result of a spontaneous altercation, rumour suggests it was related to gangland affairs. Some old-timers indicate that Rocco Perri, the ruthless mob boss known as "Canada's Al Capone," was associated with the Queen's Hotel speakeasy. Rocco was famous for saying, "I don't kill people; they die all by themselves." Could it be that this ruthless man had a hand in the slaying?

The story goes that a bootlegging deal had gone sour. The individual responsible for the mistake slipped into the Queen's late one night to beg forgiveness, but the mob boss was not a forgiving man. They exchanged heated words. Suddenly, stepping out of the darkness, three thugs loomed over the frightened bootlegger. The gangster decided to make an example of his unfortunate employee. He clearly did not tolerate mistakes. Rocco's henchmen went about their murderous business, and the screams of the victim grew louder with each hurled fist. Then there was silence.

Who exactly this victim was, and the circumstance under which he died, has never been determined. No corpse was ever found to lend credence to the story, but that doesn't necessarily mean anything. After all, Rocco himself mysteriously disappeared and was presumed murdered in 1945, yet his body has never been recovered. The remains of both men, Rocco Perri and the Queen's unknown victim, likely lie at the bottom of a lake or buried deep in a field.

After Prohibition ended, it soon became obvious that the Queen's Hotel would never be the grand hotel it once was. The decades that followed were not kind to the establishment. Neglected, weathered, and rotting, it seemed to sag under the weight of its notorious reputation. Strange noises were heard within and, more than once, individuals claimed to hear the sounds of angry voices. Their words were indistinguishable, but their threatening intent was all too clear to those present.

In later years it was said that when the hotel interior was cast in darkness, you could hear someone walking across the floorboards, the steps making a very distinct sound. They were heavy, laboured, and loud. The footsteps would come towards startled witnesses and seemingly halt right in front of them. So clear was the sound that many people hesitatingly reached out into the inky darkness to find out if someone was standing before them. In some cases, the heavy-footed walker was so close you could smell his booze-drenched breath warmly caressing your face. And yet, there was never any one there. Anyone material, that is.

As one might expect, these encounters always instilled fear in the witnesses. But more than that, it filled them with an overwhelming dread, as if they were sharing the final emotions of a condemned man. It was clear that the fear and the pain, which the spirit had endured in this world, had followed him into the next.

At long last, however, the poor soul found peace. When the property was purchased by the Toronto Dominion Bank in 1970, the Queen's Hotel was in such a dismal condition that it was promptly demolished. With the destruction of the building, whatever shackles bound the ghost of the Queen's Hotel to our world were severed. As far as we know, there have been no unexplained phenomena in the new bank building.

# Chapter 5
# The Spectral Soldier and his Eternal Watch

There are times we tend to forget or to take for granted those who died in battle long ago. But some places — haunted battlefields and military installations, for example — don't allow us the luxury of burying the pain and suffering of war. Here the voices of the past continue to echo, forcing us to come to grips with the destructive nature of war, reminding us, often in the most startling ways, that we should take the time to think about those who gave their lives in defence of our nation.

In the town of Penetanguishene, lying in a secluded inlet on the shores of storm-tossed Georgian Bay is a recreated navy base. This base protected the Upper Great Lakes from U.S. aggression for more than three decades in the

Private Drury still stands sentinel over the
officers' quarters at Discovery Harbour.

early nineteenth century. Today, it's a living-history museum
known as Discovery Harbour, where costumed guides bring
naval history to life in all its deck-swabbing glory. And though
he isn't officially a staff member, James Drury has made
a name for himself as the most "senior" guide on the site.
Drury is the only one with first-hand knowledge of the era in
question. After all, he's been there since the 1830s.

The base itself dates back two decades earlier, to the
height of the War of 1812. The Battle of Lake Erie in 1813, in
which Commodore Oliver Hazzard Perry's squadron hum-
bled the mighty British Royal Navy, drastically shifted the
naval balance of power in the Great Lakes. The English realized they needed a new fleet on Lake Huron, as well as a protected anchorage in which to build and base it. Various sites

were looked at, but the natural harbour at Penetanguishene was ultimately selected. Work began in the winter of 1813.

Construction continued even after the conflict ended in 1814. Britain vowed never again to fall prey to U.S. hostility. The 1820s were the base's heyday, at which time it was home to half a dozen naval vessels and more than 100 navy and army personnel. But the site, one of the more remote postings anywhere in the Empire, was isolated from civilization. Life there was marked by boredom, disease, depravation, and all too often, suicide. It's no wonder that it became home to several restless souls. Private James Drury is the ghost of a young soldier who was garrisoned at the base in the late 1830s.

New Year's Eve of 1839, a particularly blustery winter night, found the lad shivering at his post outside the officers' quarters. The officers themselves were all in town celebrating, but for Drury there was little to be joyful about. He was cold, tired, and thoroughly miserable. Private Drury, figuring that with everybody celebrating there was little chance of getting caught, disobeyed orders by entering the officers' quarters to find shelter from the cold and wind. He further broke regulations by helping himself to a bottle of sherry he found inside. Being young and from an impoverished background, Drury had never before tasted sherry nor had he experienced the intoxicating effects of alcohol. He liked the taste, as well as the smooth way it slid down his throat, and he found that it created embers of warmth in his belly that helped him recover from the chill that was upon him. One glass turned into two and two into three. "Just one more, to steel myself against the cold," he kept telling himself. Soon, the bottle was empty and the young soldier thoroughly drunk. Only then did Private Drury stagger back to his post.

Sadly, he succumbed to the lethal combination of alcohol poisoning and severe exposure, and he lay alone in the snow in the bone-numbing cold until at last he died. He was found the next morning, stiffly slumped against the door of the officers' quarters. Salvation had been just a turn of the door handle away. Yet, he had been too drunk and too weak from the cold to save himself.

The base's commanding officer couldn't possibly have known, when he assigned Private Drury to guard duty that night that it would be an eternal watch for the young soldier. Almost two centuries have passed, and he has never been relieved of that lonely post.

Since his death in 1839, Private Drury never ventures far from the officers' quarters, but he has made his presence known to generations of staff and tourists alike. Among other things, he is known for stealing wine glasses and whiskey bottles. Curators believe he is attempting to prevent others from falling prey to the devil drink, as he once did. Many people claim to hear heavy footsteps in the building, even when no one is there. And there are always other strange unaccountable noises in the officers' quarters that have no natural source and must, by definition, be termed supernatural.

Curators have reported seeing Drury. He'll be spotted sitting on one of the officer's beds and then, as if he knows that he's been caught somewhere off-limits to a mere private, he simply vanishes. Startled witnesses are left wondering if their eyes have a played a trick on them. But then they notice the bed. The mattress is left dented as though someone had been there moments before. Other times, after the base is closed at night, staff sometimes see, out of the corners of their eyes, what they take to be a tourist walking through the building. When they approach to see if the tourist is lost or unaware that the museum is closed, he disappears before their eyes.

"When you're alone in there, you hear these noises and know Private Drury is walking about," says one university student who found summer employment at Discovery Harbour. "It kind of creeps you out. I've been scared a few times." One time in particular stands out in this young man's mind. It was a fairly typical summer afternoon. The sun was shining warmly and there was not a cloud in the sky. The museum was alive with the usual complement of tourists and staff. In other words, it was not a time when you expect to experience ghostly activity. A young boy standing alone in front of the officers' quarters caught the attention of the student guide. The boy just stood there, glued to the spot, intently staring at something in the doorway. He seemed confused and a little frightened, so the guide approached to check up on him. There was nothing unusual in the entrance, at least as far as the guide could tell, and when he asked the child if he was alright — the child just nodded absently — almost as if in a trance.

As this was happening, the boy's parents came over and asked their son if he wanted to go inside the building. He shook his head. The parents tried to coax him in, figuring he was just a little intimidated by the old building. But still he refused. Nothing they said could convince him to enter the officers' quarters. The parents, quite perplexed, asked him why he wouldn't go inside. "Because the man doesn't want us to," the young boy said as he pointed at the seemingly empty doorway. By this time, the guide was completely unnerved and had to excuse himself. "That was it for me, man. Too weird. And it got me thinking if there were times when Private Drury didn't want us in the building either, but we just weren't sensitive enough to know it."

There have been numerous other times when the past and present have collided at Discovery Harbour. For example, in his book *True Canadian Ghost Stories*, John Robert Colombo tells about a letter he received. It was sent to him by Rosemary Vyvyan, then the historical planner at the living history museum. In her letter she relates strange happenings she experienced in the officers' quarters. While not particularly horrific, they are unsettling nonetheless, enough to leave one questioning one's sanity.

"Another incident occurred several years ago when I was instructed to turn off all the heat in the building to help freeze-dry a humidity problem over the winter. I did so.

About a month later I had a team of restorationists come to the site to look at the building and give me further advice for its restoration. I explained to them about the deliberate non-use of the furnaces. To my horror, when I took the group into the building, the furnace was blasting out nice warm air. To this day I have no idea who turned the furnace on and why."

As part of the restoration process, all the fragile furnishings were taken from the building over the winter. When it came time to refurnish the building in spring, one box was missing. "I searched the site for the box of things. All efforts were to no avail. You can imagine my complete shock when I went into the officers' quarters one day and the box, full of artifacts, was sitting in plain view at the top of the stairs."

Private Drury's life was interrupted by service to king and country, and was ultimately lost to it as well, albeit not in battle. Nevertheless, his ghostly presence at Discovery Harbour ensures that his sacrifice will never be forgotten.

**An Unjust Execution**
The soft wind ruffled the autumn foliage momentarily, but nothing else moved. The couple stood close, staring through the gate of the partially reconstructed War of 1812 fort, trying to detect the entity they sensed waiting within. Their eyes strained, but there was only more of what they had already seen: the foundations of former buildings, the log palisade with a Union Jack flying over it, and a dense forest encroaching upon it on all sides.

Yet one of the pair, a woman, could feel a presence here, life beyond that of nature, a spirit tormented with guilt and torn by pain. She could feel his eternal torture. Fixing her companion with a haunting gaze, her voice became rough and thick with fear, "He keeps saying, over and over again, 'Why? Why me?' He can't understand why he was hung and left to die. He was only a boy."

The shadows were lengthening and the day was beginning to fade into nightfall. The sun had already gone below the trees and it was time to leave. But later, even as the kilometres left the fort behind them, the woman could not shake the experience. She felt as dark and lost as did the ghost, and only much later did the spirit's cold embrace leave her.

Such is a typical experience at historic Fort Willow, located near the city of Barrie. It's a place that just seems made for a ghost story or two. Walking through the gates, you can almost hear the sounds of musket fire and the deafening roar of cannons, the echoes of a long ago war.

When the United States seized control of Lake Erie and severed Britain's maritime lines of communication to its isolated western forces on Lake Huron, England fell back on an old overland route that ran from Toronto to Georgian Bay. To protect the route, a small fort was hacked out of the wilderness along the banks of Willow Creek, just west of modern-day Barrie. For several years Fort Willow housed a sizable garrison that boasted log barracks, a barn, and two blockhouses, all surrounded by a defensive log palisade and trenches.

After the war's end in 1815, Britain removed its garrison, all save for one unlucky phantom soldier, who continued to stand sentry over the fort even as the forests reclaimed the site. Could he be there still, performing his duty with unflinching and undying devotion?

Those who believe so describe the ghost as a young man, probably no more than a teenager, fair and lanky, with a childlike innocence borne upon his youthful face. He is always encountered wearing a nineteenth century military uniform, and often with his head cocked to the side in a most curious fashion. Those who look carefully note that the ghost's neck is actually on an unnatural, and seemingly painful, angle.

History is largely silent about the subject, which isn't surprising as Fort Willow was an obscure and distant post. It remains widely unknown and undocumented even today. The soldier certainly wouldn't have died as a result of hostile action, since Fort Willow was far from the front lines. However, it's possible and indeed quite likely that he, and perhaps others, succumbed to physical disease or psychological debilitation. Fort Willow was, after all, described as "malarial" and as a "hellish swamp" in summer, and as "completely isolated" in winter.

Where history leaves off, legend takes over. It was the winter of 1813 – 1814 and the war was soon to end. However, few people knew this at the time, and certainly none of the soldiers stationed at Fort Willow knew it. The weather was brutal and unforgiving. Thigh-high blankets of snow made walking an almost impossible chore, and howling winds bit through the soldiers' greatcoats, chilling them to the bone. Plummeting temperatures dipped so low that it proved impossible to warm the barracks. Frostbite, pneumonia, and dysentery plagued the men.

Perhaps knowing that his end was near, the young private, who was laid low with sickness and fever, began weeping and calling desperately for his mother. Over and over again the young man cried out hoping to hear the soothing voice of his mother or feel the warmth of her arms around him. Weakened by illness, he looked more child than soldier. The need to see his mother one last time was overwhelming, and as the end neared, his sobbing became more desperate. His fever induced delirium, and one night the soldier pulled himself from his bunk and set out under the cover of darkness to be reunited with his mother. Of course, his mother was hundreds if not thousands of kilometres away, but in his incoherent state he had no way of knowing that.

When his absence was noticed, the fort's commanding officer was furious. For some unknown reason, he wasn't told about the soldier's illness. He had only been told that the young man had fled for home. No one disobeyed this captain, and certainly not a lowly private. The captain was sure that the lad had deserted his post. A search party was sent out after him. Weakened by illness and slowed by the deep cold, he hadn't gone very far before his mates caught up with him. The ill-fated soldier was tenderly carried back to the barracks.

Unfortunately, the angry captain felt that a strong message had to be sent so that others wouldn't attempt to desert. As a result, the young soldier was lashed ruthlessly, and when his strength finally gave out, a rope was knotted around his neck and he was hung up on the flagpole for all to see. Left to die, his legs kicked violently for what must have seemed like an eternity as his body weight gradually strangled him. It was a slow and agonizing way to perish. In a chilling exit, the young man cried out in a most mournful and haunting way — "Why?" — as his body twitched for the last time.

For several days the young man's body remained hanging from the pole. When it was finally brought down, its ghastly appearance sent bone-chilling shudders through the other soldiers. His eyes were eaten away and, with his neck broken, his head rolled grotesquely to one side. The corpse was quickly buried and forgotten. A few months later the garrison pulled out, never to return.

But today, beneath the partially reconstructed palisade and through the eerie woods, the ghostly soldier silently continues his patrol. For those perceptive enough to see him or to sense his presence, he invokes sadness and fear. These ethereal feelings are no doubt reflections of those which the ghost himself experienced as he was unjustly sentenced to death.

Almost two centuries have passed, and yet, the young soldier cannot rest. He remains steadfast at Fort Willow.

Perhaps to prove that he did not desert his post all those years ago — he continues to stand guard — possibly for all eternity.

## The Mournful Ghosts of Mutchinbacker Mill

Since earliest times, spirits have been associated with water, whether a placid pool, a turbulent river, a majestic waterfall, or even a ground well. Some of these apparitions are said to be the ghosts of people who have drowned. It is often supposed that the spirits are seeking to entice other helpless victims into joining them in their watery graves. Other ghosts are thought to be more sad than malicious. The latter category are generally assumed to be those who have lost loved ones in the water's depths and who are forever tied to our world in a vain effort to find their lost loves. One particular river in Ontario's Muskoka region plays host to both types of ghosts.

The Rosseau River runs a rather placid 18 kilometres from Long Lake before finally pouring into Lake Rosseau's Mutchinbacker Bay through a tempestuous chute. While the water slows to a trickle during dry summers, each spring the river thunders past in an angry maelstrom of churning water. It is most impressive in its sheer unbridled power. It was this power that fed the mill located at the river's mouth, and delivered the logs from the distant interior to the awaiting saws. Lumbermen depended upon the river for their livelihood. They also feared and respected it as more than one man lost his life in the spring drives.

For more than half a century, these drives were a familiar sight in the Muskokas. Every spring, thousands of old-growth trees, which had been felled the previous winter, were sent barrelling down the swollen rivers to accumulate in the lakes below, often packing the waterways so tightly that one could literally walk from one shore to the next without getting one's feet wet.

Today, a century later, the same rivers and lakes are eerily silent at this time of year. The timber industry has long since passed the region by and most of the mills have left little tangible evidence of their existence. One exception, however, is the sawmill at Mutchinbacker Bay where a devoted young woman ensures that these once vital industries do not entirely fade from our memories. She is neither historian nor curator, and doesn't so much relate history as reflect it. For this woman is, or rather was, very much a part of the memories her presence serves to preserve. She is a shadow of the past, someone intimately connected to the frenzied milling activity that took place in Mutchinbacker Bay well over 100 years ago. Through her troubled spirit we can still hear the buzz of the saw blades and smell the scent of freshly cut wood.

Lumbering on the Rosseau River began in 1865, when Peter Mutchinbacker built a mill at the base of the Rosseau River rapids, and continued unabated for 80 years. It finally closed in the mid-1940s after the supply of harvestable lumber had been exhausted. But that would not be the last the world would hear of the mill on Mutchinbacker Bay. The ghostly woman, garbed in pioneer dress, is occasionally seen

Does the gurgling of the water at Rosseau Falls disguise the
sobs of a spectral woman mourning the loss of her beloved?

along the riverbank. Her presence provides an intangible
and startling link to the past and, though she doesn't reveal
herself often, her appearances are frequent enough to refresh
receding memories of the area's milling heritage.

No one knows who the young woman might be, or
exactly when her story began. Strange things were first
reported along the Rosseau River soon after the turn of the
twentieth century. People reported seeing the smoky image
of a lovely lady walking along the river or sitting patiently on
a rock alongside the rapids. In either case, her gaze is always
firmly rooted upriver. And it never wavers. It's as if her heart,
her entire being, is focused on something beyond our vision,

something farther north and deep within the forest. Anyone who sees her knows immediately that she is not a part of our world, for she seems to be walking ... not on ... but just inches above the rocks.

The spectral woman, who appears more often in the springtime and during periods of the full moon, is described as being little more than a teenager. Her brown hair is pulled back in a bun framing a lovely young face, and she wears a long dress that is narrow at the waist and lacy around the collar (in the style of the Victorian era). An unnatural mist that seems to coil from the water, like ghostly tendrils, often coincides with her appearances.

As lovely as the young woman might be, her beauty is marred by a sadness that seems to weigh upon her. Her sorrow seems almost tangible, and it's likely that this powerful emotion keeps her soul bound to the river. Legend says her spirit is searching for the love of her earthly life, a logger who met an untimely demise, either by felling trees over the winter or by drowning during the spring drive. Witnesses claim to see a pleading expression on her face, as if she desperately wants help in finding her long-lost love. In addition, witnesses also report a heart-wrenching despair in her gaze.

While history doesn't record the circumstances of her life, one tale hints at a possible series of events. It may have been that her parents promised the young woman without her consent to a lumberman. The marriage, on the surface, seemed loveless. But to the young woman's surprise, as time passed, she found herself no longer resenting her husband, but rather falling in love with him. Tragically, he died before she was ever able to let him know of her change of heart. Her spirit comes to the falls today, as perhaps she did in life, hoping to connect with her husband and once again feel his arms around her.

Even more disturbing than the ghostly image of the distraught woman, however, are the spine-chilling sounds that mix with the natural cacophony of the night. The most distinctive of these noises is a gurgling sound (somewhat like the sound that comes from the back of your throat when gargling with mouthwash). It lasts only for a few hair-raising seconds, and then it is gone, but in those brief moments it causes one's skin to crawl and it leaves people thoroughly shaken. A rational mind might pass it off as water frothing in the river, though others believe it to be the disembodied sounds of a man drowning. Perhaps the sounds are made by the man for whose arrival our spectral lady patiently awaits.

Sadly, it seems that her vigil will be eternal, because the logs that would have heralded the arrival of her beloved have long since stopped flowing down the Rosseau River. And so she remains, an unwilling link to the past. Her forlorn spirit reflects not only a time before the cruel hands of fate tore her idyllic life apart, but also an era — a time long ago — when the now-tranquil river was the centre of a frenzied and dangerous industry.

# *Chapter 6*
# Lost Treasures

**A**t one point or another in life most of us have dreamed about finding buried treasure. To the majority it might just be a dream; to others it's a life-long search. But some treasures are meant to stay hidden. They defy all efforts at recovery — lost, perhaps, forever. And then there are those riches that probably should have remained undiscovered, treasures that carry with them horrible curses. In finding these treasures a simple dream often turns into a formidable nightmare.

Ontario is home to both kinds of treasures, those that bring bountiful fortunes, and those that, in the end, bring nothing but misfortune. At some point we've all imagined stumbling upon a buried cache of treasure, finding a price-less heirloom in the attic, or inheriting a fabulous fortune.

Money, it seems, is an almost universal aspiration. Wealth solves all problems. Or does it?

## The Curse of the Ring

When Ontario's Mrs. Park acquired the diamond ring that had belonged to Mary, Queen of Scots, she must have been overwhelmed with delight. After all, it was worth a fortune. But the ring brought with it unexpected complications in the form of a deadly curse, the origins of which date back to the execution of Queen Mary over 400 years ago. Maybe diamonds aren't a girl's best friend after all?

Mary Stuart knew the time had come for her to pay the price for plotting to assassinate her cousin, Queen Elizabeth I, and take over the throne of England. Death now awaited her. There would be no pardon, no leniency. The axe was already sharpened for her beheading. Mary, Queen of Scots, a woman who inspired both utter devotion and spiteful hatred, was publicly executed in February 1587. It took three swings of the axe to complete the bloody task.

It's said that Mary died with dignity — but not without malice. Prior to her execution, she placed a curse on her crown jewels, swearing that no one would ever profit by her death. The venom of her words and the tragedy of her life and death infused her jewels with evil auras, auras that have "a fatal influence upon the lives of people who become possessed of them."

One of the accursed jewels, a diamond ring of unsurpassed beauty, likely rests today in Ontario. Its route to Canada took over three centuries to complete and was not accomplished without considerable bloodshed and tears. A trail of tragedy followed its every move.

The beautiful but ill-fated Mary Stuart had led a troubled existence from the very beginning. She was born second in line to the throne of England, after her cousin Elizabeth. But to most Catholic Englishmen she represented a far more appealing monarch than did the unwed Protestant Elizabeth. Mary, therefore, became fuel for the religious and political fires that engulfed Britain in the sixteenth century. There were multiple conspiracies to overthrow Elizabeth during this period. Mary was at the heart of many of them.

Mary was hardly an innocent. She was capable of devious plotting and murderous deeds if she thought these would advance her self-interest. Her second husband, Lord Darnley, was killed under suspicious circumstances, and the man thought guilty of the murders, the Earl of Bothwell, became her third husband not long thereafter.

Shadowy dealings such as this were typical of this ambitious woman. But it was too much for the nobles of Scotland, who forced Mary to flee into exile in England. For the next 20 years, many of which were spent under house arrest, she would play a central role in both real and imagined conspiracies aimed at deposing Queen Elizabeth. Suspicions about her involvement finally culminated in 1586 when she was caught, red-handed, plotting to assassinate the queen. The sentence for her crime was death.

Her extensive collection of fine jewellery had already been bequeathed to others by the time of her execution. All that remained in her possession was an exquisite Italian Renaissance diamond ring. Just before she climbed the scaffold in Fotheringay Castle where she would die, Mary paused and gave a small jewel casket to one of her handmaidens (history has mistakenly identified this woman as Mary Carmichael). This case contained the last earthly possession of the Queen of Scots, her diamond ring.

If the folklore does indeed have a basis in reality, then the most likely candidate to receive the ring was not Mary Carmichael, but was the doomed queen's handmaiden, Mary Fleming. Tragedy certainly marred her later life. It started when her husband died after a long illness. During his illness and after his death Mary was badgered by representatives of the Scottish king to turn over the jewels that had been given to her by Queen Mary. They claimed the jewellery belonged to the state, not the monarch. One thing after another plagued Mary Fleming's life, including her second marriage to George Meldum of Fyvie, which was an unhappy one. Then, to top it all off, she lived the last of her days in Fyvie Castle, long considered one of Scotland's most haunted manors. Her death in 1600 was probably a release from a dismal existence.

No matter. Whether it was Mary Fleming or whether it was Mary Carmichael, the recipient of the ring could not have suspected that an evil aura hung over the beautiful gift. In fact, none of those who later came into possession of Mary Stuart's jewels initially suspected anything out of the ordinary. But over time, the dark nature of the jewels emerged. Fortunes were mysteriously lost. A man shot himself for no apparent reason. Odd deaths befell family members and unexplained mishaps stalked wearers of the jewellery with uncomfortable frequency.

Legend says the years that followed were difficult ones for Mary. As if the horror of seeing her mistress and dear friend beheaded wasn't enough for one woman to bear, the black nature of the ring began to ruin her life and cloud her mind. She suffered from icy chills, unexplained ills, and crippling depressions.

It wasn't long before various and subsequent owners of Mary Stuart's royal jewels, including Mary Carmichael, came to hold the jewels responsible for their ills. In an attempt to distance themselves from the curse, they locked the valuables away. "They were hidden in secret cupboards in British country houses; they were buried under piles of ancient lumber and among time-stained, mouldy books; they were hidden under old records in the archives rooms of English castles; and yet somehow have forced themselves into the modern day, often with dire and fatal consequences to those who have bought them for a few dollars in auction rooms or in country junk shops."

No one knows exactly when the diamond ring re-emerged, but during the late nineteenth century it was in the hands of the aristocratic Roddam family, a family with ancestral ties to Mary Stuart. In 1905, Admiral Roddam of the Royal Navy bequeathed the ring to Mrs. William Park, a Canadian descendant of the Queen of Scots. But if Admiral Roddam was attempting to free his family of Mary's curse, he wasn't entirely successful. Exactly 10 years later, a son was killed in World War I when an unexplained explosion sunk his ship at anchor in Malta. A coincidence, perhaps, but a chilling one.

Mrs. Park resided in Ontario's Durham Township. She was a simple woman far removed from the wealth and splendour of her famous ancestor, so to her the valuable ring she inherited must have seemed spectacular. She treated it as a prized heirloom. Did she know of the dark curse embedded in the stone? It seems unlikely.

But she may have discovered it for herself over time. Folklore says that soon after acquiring the diamond ring unexplained phenomenon began to pay Mrs. Park regular visits, and she was tormented by odd mishaps and reversals of fortune. We won't ever know for sure, because she passed away in 1934 having never documented her experiences or fears.

As for the malicious ring, the last anyone heard it was in the hands of a wealthy Toronto woman. It's a dubious treasure to say the least. With such a tragic history behind this unique piece of jewellery, it would take someone awfully brave to chance wearing the ring ... wouldn't it? Perhaps the curse will have worn off when the next person inherits the ring. Stay tuned.

## The Hidden Treasure of Jesse James

Ontario is rich with tales of unmarked mines, lost army pay-chests, shipwrecks, and buried treasures. It's a big province, and there is apparently a lot of loot to be found, if one knows where to look. Some tales, surely, are pure fiction. Others have an undeniable historical basis. And then there are those that occupy the shadow world, the in-between, a place where fact and fantasy mix and mingle until they're nearly impossible to separate.

A treasure reputed to lay hidden near Shelburne occupies this murky nether region. Somewhere in an unmarked field is a fortune in stolen money, the ill-gotten gains of the notorious outlaw, Jesse Woodson James.

Jesse James, one of the best-known outlaws of the American West, was a murderous bandit who was the terror of banks and railroads for almost 20 years. He fascinated the public and they eagerly devoured his exploits, which were reported in newspapers and immortalized in dime novels. There has never been a gunslinger as widely reviled nor as greatly admired as Jesse James.

Jesse James was born in 1847. By the time he was 17, he and his older brother Frank were learning the tools of their future trade while serving with Bloody Bill Anderson's raiders in the Civil War. When the war ended, the James brothers refused to hang up their guns, and used them instead to hold up banks and rob trains. Nobody knows exactly how many robberies the James Gang pulled off or how much money they robbed at the point of a gun. At least two dozen heists are definitively linked to Jesse James, many of which netted his gang thousands of dollars. One example is the $10,000 lifted from a bank in Huntington, West Virginia, in 1875.

On April 3, 1882, his 17-year crime spree came to a violent end when Robert Ford, a member of his own gang who wanted to claim the $10,000 price on Jesse James's head, shot him from behind. He died, but the legend of this notorious robber lives on, sometimes in unlikely places.

Shelburne, Ontario, is a long way from Jesse's old stomping grounds in Clay County, Missouri, yet his legend is firmly embedded in local folklore. It seems the outlaw was a frequent visitor to these parts during his short life. He was in the habit of slipping across the border whenever the heat back home grew too intense. According to Wayne Thompson, the curator at the Dufferin County Museum, Jesse's frequent visits have been well documented in newspaper reports.

The outlaw was a houseguest of the Bailey family, who were modest farmers in the area with close ties to the James clan. The Baileys were originally from Clay County, Missouri, and like most residents of those parts where loyalty to family and friends was respected above all other considerations, they were highly protective of the James boys. Mrs. Bailey even claimed to have been a childhood friend of Jesse James.

"She went to school with him," notes Alison Hird of the Dufferin County Museum, "and in her Shelburne newspaper columns always wrote that he was a good boy."

At one point, Jesse James figured his Clay County haunts were becoming too well known by outlaws and lawmen alike, so he decided to bury his illegally acquired wealth in a safer location. The elusive bandit made his way north from Missouri, evading the law for hundreds of kilometres, and slipped anonymously into Canada. He arrived at the Bailey farm, wearied from the road and riding a horse heavily laden with money.

Then late one night, with the darkness masking his actions from prying eyes, James dug a pit in the middle of a field and buried his money. This stash, cleverly removed from his usual stomping grounds, well hidden, and under the watchful protection of loyal friends, was about as secure as he could make it. The location was so secret that no member of the gang, except for his brother Frank, was trusted with the knowledge — and for good reason — the booty was reported to consist of as much as one million dollars.

One story has the treasure's location marked with a *Z* slashed across a tree in a Zorro-like fashion. This seemingly fanciful twist to the legend may actually have some truth to it. Jesse's beloved wife, whom he was utterly devoted to, was named Zee Mimms. The treasure was safe all right, so safe that it remains undiscovered more than a century later. The fact that Bob Ford killed the outlaw before he could return to Canada to collect his money may be the only reason Jesse did not dig it up himself. There have been those over the years who have attempted to locate and recover the loot, but always without success. The most notable effort occurred in the 1970s when more than a hectare was torn up, in vain, by a backhoe.

To date, no one has discovered the cache. That can mean only one of two things. Either the story is a fabrication or the lost treasure of Jesse James is still out there waiting to be uncovered. As with almost everything about the legendary outlaw, truth is shrouded in folklore. So, if during your travels in the Shelburne area, you should come across a tree with a *Z* etched into it, don't just walk away. Think for a moment. It just might mark a stash of loot that has been waiting 125 years to be found.

### Treasure and Treason

With dawn approaching, John Lyon could finally breathe a sigh of relief. The night before, he had watched with fear and trepidation as the U.S. warships pulled away from York (Toronto) Harbour, taking with them the soldiers that had occupied Ontario's capital for the past week. With his bene-factors no longer there to protect him, he knew he would face repercussions for having aided the enemy. But Lyon also knew that he couldn't be prosecuted if there was no evidence against him. So the traitor had raced home to hide his ill-gotten goods before dawn. Working feverishly, he dumped hundreds of farming implements and several casks of coin (bribery intended to woo settlers over to the U.S. camp) into a secret cache. A millpond possibly? His treasure was well and truly hidden.

Perhaps it was hidden too well. Neither John Lyons, nor anyone else for that matter, has ever recovered the gold or the goods. The hoard has rested ever since in the same place it was hastily dropped that night in 1813.

It is ironic that the majority of settlers in Upper Canada in the early nineteenth century originally hailed from the United States, not Britain. Loyalists, who remained true to the Crown during the American Revolution, were the first wave of settlers to Upper Canada in the late 1700s. But soon they were vastly outnumbered by Americans lured to the area not by political idealism, but rather by a simple desire for land. Indeed, it was estimated that upon the outbreak of the War of 1812, almost half of Upper Canada's population was American or of American parentage. This was naturally a cause for concern for the British authorities. Would these newcomers remain true to their adopted country in the wake of hostilities with the United States?

As it turned out, such fears were largely unfounded, and most settlers remained loyal to their adopted home. But there were exceptions to this rule, men whose sympathies lay with the United States and who aided and abetted the enemy. John Lyon of Thornhill (a community just north of Toronto) was one such traitor.

John Lyon was born on Long Island, New York, in 1769, but immigrated to Upper Canada in 1796 and settled along Yonge Street in what is now Thornhill (where the Thornhill Golf Course is now located). In 1801 he built the area's first sawmill, later adding a gristmill and distillery. In addition to being a successful businessman, he was also a public servant. Lyon was named "path master," whose responsibility it was to keep the roads in good order. Everything up until this point suggests that Lyon was a loyal and content citizen of the British Empire. However, the ultimate test of his loyalties came a year after the United States declared war on Britain and began successive invasions into Upper Canada in 1812.

On April 27, 1813, a U.S. naval squadron appeared off York and began landing hundreds of soldiers. Despite a brisk defence by the handful of British troops protecting the town, the invaders soon seized control of York. Wholesale plunder followed. It was at this point that John Lyon demonstrated his dubious loyalty.

In a deposition later made out before Justice of the Peace, Thomas Ridout, William Knott declared (August 17), "On Sunday the first day of August last; while the Enemy's forces were in York, he saw John Lyon of the Township of Vaughan, distiller, drawing with his wagon Public Stores down to the Water Side for the Enemy, he saw no appearance of compulsion, and for all that it appeared Lyon did it voluntarily."

The Americans sacked the government stores and plundered the town, and it seems that John Lyon assisted them in bringing the ransacked goods down to the waterfront for transfer to waiting ships. Whatever goods the Americans could not take with them (mostly farming implements) were distributed to the settlers that had assisted them during their occupation of York. The Americans hoped that this demonstration of goodwill and generosity would cause the townsfolk to question their loyalty to Great Britain. The U.S. forces withdrew before all the goods could be handed out, however, leaving Lyon with a vast hoard of stolen government property on his hands. To avoid prosecution, he concealed the goods either in his millpond or the Don River nearby. This much is established history.

But folklore has more to add to the story. It seems that the U.S. commander, General Dearborn, left a considerable sum of gold coins in the care of John Lyon, money intended to bribe the citizens of York in exchange for loyalty and action over the next few months. A few coins quietly slipped into a palm here and there might have a profound impact on the war. For example, farmers might fail to deliver grain harvests, a commodity in great demand to feed British troops in the field. Or soldiers could waver on the field of battle. Also, officials just might become negligent in their duties. In total, the money may have amounted to $2000, the equivalent of $800,000 today (this at a time when a skilled craftsman might make $100 a year).

Lyon was never found with the money in his possession. This would have been proof positive of his guilt, and he would likely have faced capital punishment for treason. Clearly, the coins, which were either hidden in the bottom of several whiskey barrels or in an ironclad U.S. Navy payroll chest, must have been stashed away. At the same time, however, Lyon would have had to keep them near at hand and readily accessible, in the event he had to make use of the money in the name of U.S. interests. The millpond on his property was a convenient and logical hiding place.

John Lyon never had the opportunity to make use of the treasure, nor would he ever answer for his treasonous actions. A few short months later, with the war still raging — he died suddenly — and somewhat suspiciously, at the age of 44 years. With him went the secret of the loot's location. Surely, with such a lucrative prize, people must have searched for the missing treasure. But, as far as we know, their efforts have all been in vain. To date, nothing has been recovered from the water — no gold coins, no pay chest, not even the farm implements.

It's now been almost 200 years, and the mystery of why John Lyon acted against his adopted country and what became of his Judas gold has never been solved. John Lyon's motive died with him in 1813 — but presumably the money that was his reward still lies out there — awaiting an eager treasure hunter.

# Chapter 7
# Mysteries of the Deep

T he Titanic. The Flying Dutchman. The Bermuda Triangle. Some of our greatest mysteries are tied to water, and surely the answers to these enduring enigmas, assuming answers exist, lie deep below the surface. Those hardy souls who made their living aboard ships were a superstitious lot and, to a man, they respected the power of nature. They knew that the ocean only reluctantly gives up its secrets.

Ontario may be located in the middle of Canada, but the province is far from landlocked. In fact, it's bounded on almost every border by water — the Great Lakes to the south and west, the Ottawa River to the east, and the Hudson Bay to the north. Ontario also boasts thousands of smaller lakes and rivers, earning it the nickname Lake O' Lakes. It is hardly surprising that Ontario has her share of maritime secrets.

## Maid of the Mist

Niagara Falls is recognized as one of the great natural wonders of the world, a place of spellbinding beauty and tempestuous majesty. Millions of tourists visit Niagara Falls every year, making it the most famous waterfall in the world. Many come away changed forever. Some never leave. Standing next to these falls is an unforgettable experience.

Ever since French explorers first laid their eyes on the waterfall in the seventeenth century, we've viewed Niagara Falls with awe. The roar of the crashing water seems to pull people irresistibly towards it, and it is difficult to cast off its enchantment. Occultist Aleister Crowley alluded to this power when, after visiting Niagara Falls in 1906, he wrote, "My dearest destiny would be to live and die within them."

Long ago, a Native woman, known to us today as the Maid of the Mist, the namesake of the famous tourist boat, must have felt the same way. Her story is among the most hauntingly beautiful of the numerous tales tied to Niagara Falls, a tale both tragic and romantic.

The falls holds special meaning for her people. The word "Niagara" is derived from *nia-gara*, the last remaining word of the Neutral Indians who dwelt in this region until the mid-1600s. In their tongue, the word means "mighty thunderer" or "thunder of water," an apt description of the waterfalls that have made Niagara famous. Native people regard the river with reverence. They consider the spirit of the Niagara, a god-like being called He-No the Thunderer who lives in a cave behind the waterfalls, to be the embodiment of elemental power.

Anyone who visits the falls can easily see why. Water plunges over the crest at speeds up to 32 kilometres per hour with such force that, over the centuries, it has worn a plunge pool 52 metres deep below the falls. Every second, an incredible 2,832 cubic metres of water thunder over the rocks. In the days before the Europeans decided to shape the river for their own interests, by diverting water for hydroelectric generation, the falls thundered with an even greater power. As much as 5,720 cubic metres of water poured over the falls every second, at speeds in excess of 50 kilometres per hour.

The Maid of the Mist was enthralled by the beauty of Niagara Falls. Her name was Lelawala and she was the daughter of a chief. She was a beautiful Neutral Indian maiden, a young headstrong girl barely in her teens who clashed repeatedly with her father. The chief was a conservative man who expected that his word be obeyed and his demands unfailingly met. Lelawala's most dramatic clashes with her father were over her suitors. The chief expected her to marry a man of considerable stature, one who would enhance the family line. Lelawala recoiled at this demand.

The young maiden saw things quite differently than did her father, for she knew the power and allure of romantic love. A friendship with a certain Neutral man had blossomed into love, and it was he that Lelawala intended to wed. Many times, the young lovers strolled along the banks of the Niagara River, stopping to hold each other at a special spot overlooking the falls. To Lelawala, the fact that the brave's family held no power or influence in the tribe was of little concern. She knew this was the man she wanted to be with. And so, with the innocence of a young woman in love, she approached her father and asked his permission to marry the young man.

Not surprisingly, her father refused. What's more, he forbade Lelawala from ever seeing her beloved again. He began hastily preparing for a wedding with a more suitable groom, a groom of his own choosing. Lelawala cried and begged for her father to relent, telling him that she could never live with any man other than her beloved. But her father had an iron will. His decision was final.

The thought of marrying a man she did not care for made her despondent and desperate. Once passion had touched her she couldn't bear to live in a loveless union and — seeing no other way out — she vowed to let death be her escape. When the moon was high in the night sky, Lelawala slipped away from her longhouse and crept down to the edge of the Niagara River, where she pushed a canoe into the water. There was little need to paddle. The pull of the mighty falls took hold of the canoe and began dragging Lelawala to her fate. She knew in her heart that she had made the right decision, and as her canoe plummeted over the falls a great peace settled over her.

She was pulled down the 54-metre cliff and was lost forever within the mist that forms at the base of the falls. Presumably, Lelawala's canoe crashed upon the rocks, but her body was never found. Her spirit, however, was rescued from an eternity of aimless wandering by He-No the Thunderer. He was taken aback by her beauty and courage, and was moved to give the tragic woman a home in his cave behind the falls. She has been known ever since as the Maiden of the Mists.

Together, He-No and Lelawala provide a constant supernatural presence at Niagara Falls. On sunny days, many visitors have claimed to see the Native maiden floating in and out of the mists that shroud the base of the falls. Others see her image in the rainbow that arches over the river.

But the beauty and wonder of Niagara Falls is not a welcome and predictable experience for everyone. For some, the mournful beckoning of the falls is so overwhelming that they catapult themselves to their deaths. Suicide. Do they feel the same overwhelming peace that Lelawala experienced or do they suddenly realize what they have done? Either way, once within the mists their spirits are met by Lelawala, and welcomed into her refuge behind the falls. Each and every one of these driven souls, each possessed by his or her own tragic circumstance, becomes a part of the legend and legacy of Niagara Falls. And each takes a place alongside the tragic Maid of the Mist.

**The Last Voyageur**

Lakes and rivers often seem to have an unexplained eeriness to them. No wonder. The mystery and intrigue associated with them are, invariably, kept hidden well below the surface.

In the autumn of 1812, just a few months after the United States invaded Canada, a small band of French-Canadian voyageurs serving the British Crown struggled to complete an exhausting maritime journey in the face of northern Ontario's harsh November weather. When they finally paddled into their destination, they were relieved that only one man had perished along the way. A few months later, they were discharged from service. The remaining men returned to their previous lives, and for them the war was finished.

For that one voyageur, however, the lone casualty of the desperate late-season voyage, there was no such closure. He was never discharged. He never returned home. And for him, the war will never be over. Instead, this tragic figure languishes in a tormented state along the French River. When the autumn days turn crisp and the nights gather frost, when shadows grow long upon the land and the waters grow dark and cold, the voyageur's spirit rises from his lonely, watery grave. In this haunting fashion, he celebrates each anniversary of his death.

In October, just a few months after the war's opening shots were fired, the North West Company (NWC) raised a military unit from among its employees, known as the Corps of Canadian Voyageurs, and offered it for active service. It was their task to keep supplies moving from Montreal to the western outposts and to maintain the economically vital fur trade throughout the war.

Despite performing admirably, the Corps of Canadian Voyageurs was disbanded on March 14, 1813. But the voyageurs (or at least one voyageur) didn't simply fade into the mists of time. A phantom voyageur haunts the French River, lingering eternally, and by all accounts angrily, along the waterway's rugged shores. His torment is the result of a gross misdeed. According to folklore, when the men of the corps went their separate ways they took with them a dark secret — the murder of one of their mates — none other than the young man who would become known as the Last Voyageur.

It was late autumn, and a crew of voyageurs was making one last run from Montreal to Fort Mackinac before winter set in. Pierre, as the ill-fated man might have been known, was among them and was anxious to get underway. Awaiting him at the fort on Lake Huron was his loyal Native wife, and he eagerly anticipated the passion and warmth of their forthcoming reunion. It was dangerously late in the year to be tempting fate on the waters of Lake Huron, a lake known for its relentless winter storms, but if the crew moved quickly they would likely complete the voyage before the worst of the storms arrived.

The first stretch of the journey went smoothly, but during the race down the treacherous French River an accident befell Pierre. Perhaps he fell from the canoe and was dashed against the rocks. The injury, however it occurred, was so severe that he simply couldn't be moved. To do so would be to risk his life. Only liberal doses of whiskey eased his pain. So, in the hopes that Pierre would recover, the British officer in charge of the crew ordered his men to make camp.

Pierre showed remarkable strength of will. While he didn't recover, he refused to surrender either, clinging desperately to the hope that he would see his wife once again. But with each passing day, the temperature dropped and the skies grew more ominous. Surely the commanding officer held no illusions regarding the desperate situation he faced. But to him, every life was sacred, especially those of the men under his command. He would bring all of them home safely, or none. The voyageurs, however, were more pragmatic and saw no reason to risk their lives for someone who already had one foot in the grave.

As the weather worsened, the men began to panic. They were desperate to reach their destination before the winter storms closed the lake to all sane traffic, and with each wasted day the likelihood of making the crossing without incident diminished. They pleaded with the officer to resume the journey, to sacrifice one comrade for the good of all. Each time, they were rebuked.

Then, amid gusting winds, a storm slammed into the voyageurs like a round of musket fire. Cold pelting rain stung their faces and hands, chilling the men to the bone. Fires did little to alleviate the suffering. Morale plummeted along with the temperature. Even the most hearty and enthusiastic men had their hearts frozen by the cold rain as they began despairing for their survival. Expert boatmen with years of experience on the waterways of northern Ontario they knew, even if their commanding officer didn't, that if they had any hope of reaching Fort Mackinac safely they would have to depart immediately. But they also knew that as long as Pierre had a sliver of life in him they weren't going anywhere. Crazed with desperation, they determined that Pierre must die so that they might live.

It was late at night and the camp was silent when Pierre was suddenly awakened from his restless sleep. Several dark shadows loomed over him, and then powerful hands pinned him down and smothered him. He fought like a wild man with all the strength he had left. But, weakened by injury, he was no match for his savage opponents and they managed to exhaust his remaining energy. Pierre felt ropes tightening around his wrists and ankles. The more he struggled to escape from his restraints, the more lifeless he became.

Suddenly, Pierre was in the river. The icy cold water penetrated his flesh as the river began to swallow him, and Pierre knew that his life was ending. As he took his last breath, lungs full of water, his final thought was revenge …

The next morning, just as the storm was lifting, Pierre's lifeless body was pulled from the river. His blanket, lying on the shore nearby, reeked of whiskey and the men held to their story that the poor soul must have slipped into the freezing water and drowned in a cold stupor. Noticing the red welts on the corpse's arms, and knowing Pierre had hardly been in any condition to move of his own accord, the British officer was convinced foul play was involved. He was certain the mariner had been murdered. However, he was equally aware that the death was also a warning for him — the men wanted to carry on — and they would go to desperate lengths to do so. Fearing for his own life, the officer ordered the corpse hastily buried under a pile of rocks. The group then resumed the journey westward.

While the murdered voyageur was laid to rest, his spirit was not. Just as he could not complete the journey to Fort Mackinac in life, neither would he complete the passage to the other side in death. Instead, he remains trapped in ghostly limbo. His angry and tormented spirit still walks the banks of the French River where he was slain and where, presumably, his body remains (no grave has ever been found). Usually, he manifests in late autumn, and if legend is to be believed his image slowly rises from the river's depths covered in mud and algae. Demented anger flashes in his wide-open icy cold eyes. He moves towards shore, searching for revenge against those responsible for his death.

Over the years, people travelling along the French River have claimed to hear strange sounds, low muffled moans, echoing from the water's depths or from the woods along its shores. Some have encountered unnaturally cold patches of air near the water's edge, a sure sign of a ghostly presence.

In the early 1900s, one wilderness canoeing party had an experience that would frighten even the most hardened outdoorsman. The group were warming their feet around a campfire when they began to notice a mirage-like mist clinging to the river. It hovered above the water, rising seven metres or so into the air, adding a sinister touch to an already dark and moody setting. With the unnatural fog creeping towards shore, the unnerved men hastily retired to bed.

By the middle of the night, the grey mist had swirled up onto the land. That's when the noises started. One by one, the men were woken by footsteps crunching through the brush around the perimeter of the campsite. The sounds reminded the men of the agitated pacing of a nervous animal. They were close, too close if it were a bear or wolf as the men began to suspect. But despite several sets of eyes straining into the darkness, the creature remained unseen except for brief glimpses of movement. It always remained just beyond the glow of the fire.

When the sun finally arrived at dawn and began to burn off the fog, the group ventured into the woods in search of clues to the identity of their nighttime visitor. The tracks they found about their camp were not that of a bear or wolf. They belonged to a human. Stranger still, they found evidence that the mysterious person had at one point approached within a metre of the sleeping campers, and yet no one had heard or seen a thing. By now the men were completely terrified, so they rapidly packed and moved on.

Sadly, it doesn't seem as though the restless voyageur can move on as easily. Today, almost 200 years after the voyageur's tragic death, canoers still talk of ghosts along the French River. Will Pierre ever complete his final voyage along the waters that took his life? Or is he doomed to forever linger mid-way between life and death, just as he lingered mid-way between Montreal and Fort Mackinac?

### The *Mary Ward*

Anyone who doubts that Lake Huron is as unpredictable and unforgiving as her reputation suggests will find proof to the contrary in the tragic demise of the steamship *Mary Ward*. And, as if to ensure that no one forgets this dire lesson, phantom crewmen continue to play out the frightening drama of that night to this very day.

One of the stages for this unexplainable activity was the Craigleith Boarding House. Between the tantrum-like slamming of doors and windows, unaccounted for lights, heavy disembodied footsteps, and other unnatural sounds, as well as sudden manifestations of forlorn-looking men who drifted through walls and hallways, it's a wonder that the inn had any business at all. And perhaps that's just what the ghosts wanted. They haunted the boarding house in revenge for sending the *Mary Ward* off course and its crew to their doom.

Even after the building was demolished, the spirits that frequented it found no rest. They are bound to the cold, harsh waters of Georgian Bay, doomed to replay their last deadly moments for all time. Witnesses report standing helplessly on shore during stormy autumn days and watching in horror as a rowboat is tossed about by the angry waters. Those manning the boat are seen rowing furiously for shore, but never making any headway against the winds and currents. Finally, after what seems like an eternity, but is likely no more than a few minutes, the men are suddenly swept into the frigid waters and certain death. The last agonizing screams of these lost souls cut through even the most howling of winds.

In most cases, the events look so real that onlookers are convinced they are watching a real tragedy unfold. Other times, however, it's clear that the doomed men are from another time in history. The lifeboat is old-fashioned in make and appearance, the crew are dressed in outdated clothing, and the images on the water are misty-white. In these instances, there is no question in the witnesses' minds that they are in fact seeing phantoms.

It's not just from the safety of dry land that the ghosts are seen. For more than a century flesh-and-blood sailors out on Georgian Bay have seen the spectral rowboat, and many have been so convinced of the reality of the desperate scene that they rush to aid the endangered crew. Upon arrival, however, they find the boat as well as its eight passengers missing. There is no wreckage and there are no bodies, no debris to suggest the craft has capsized or was ever there. Those who relate the incident to authorities invariably learn that no boats have been reported missing. It's only then that

The *Mary Ward*'s final voyage is a reminder
of the unpredictability of open waters.

the startled sailors realize the full horror of what it is they
have witnessed.

In one sinister tale, an attempt to rescue the doomed
crew nearly earned a concerned fisherman the same fate
as that suffered by the crew of the *Mary Ward*. Seeing the
floundering rowboat, the concerned mariner raced to render
assistance. At the last moment, he spotted the dangerous
shoals ahead and, recognizing the danger he had placed
himself in, he pulled away. At that exact moment, the ghosts
vanished from sight. The fisherman was convinced that the
drowned sailors were attempting to lure him to his death, just
as they were lured to theirs so many years before ...

By 1872, the *Mary Ward* was an old hand at the Great Lakes freight trade. For years she had plied the waters of Lake Huron, carrying all manner of goods and stopping at all ports between Sarnia and Sault Ste. Marie, always without incident. The *Mary Ward*'s final voyage was to have been as routine as those before. Her cargo was unspectacular: a few passengers, salt, oil. The route was familiar to captain and crew.

Things started off well enough. She set sail from Sarnia on the morning of November 22 and steamed uneventfully to the port of Owen Sound, where she took on more passengers and spent the night. The dawn sun illuminated the *Mary Ward* as she glided out into the open waters of Georgian Bay one more time, bound for Collingwood. The morning was pleasant and warm, despite the lateness of the season. Passengers and crew alike were in a buoyant mood. But as darkness began to creep across the bay, a severe storm approached, and the atmosphere became apprehensive.

Thunder echoed across the expanse of water, lightning crackled on the horizon, and gale-like winds whipped white-capped waves. Soon, sheets of rain began to fall from the gloomy sky, reducing visibility on the bay to near zero in mere minutes. The *Mary Ward*'s captain knew immediately that they were in for a real winter tempest and that he'd have to make for port as quickly as possible. Unfortunately, the compass suddenly malfunctioned, leaving the ship blind.

There was no way, other than by scanning for landmarks such as lighthouses, that the captain would be able to determine the correct route to Collingwood.

When a sailor aboard called out that he had spotted the Nottawasaga lighthouse, located a few kilometres west of Collingwood, everyone on board was relieved. They knew they would be safely docked in no time. Tragically, they were wrong. And for some crewmen, dead wrong.

In a terrible twist of fate, the light seen from aboard the *Mary Ward* was not from the lighthouse at all, but rather from a kerosene lantern glowing outside the Craigleith Boarding House. Now lured off course, the steamship was destined never to reach port safely. Instead, she lurched her way onto the shelf-like shoal known as Milligan's Reef, located about five kilometres offshore. The impact was so great that she split herself open upon the sand.

To save the passengers and crew, the captain knew he'd have to ask some of his men to risk their lives out in an open boat in search of assistance. Two sailors volunteered for the hazardous duty, and at 9 p.m. a lifeboat was lowered into the storm-tossed waters. No one was sure if the men would ever be seen again.

Almost miraculously, the sailors managed to make their way to Collingwood the next morning. They arranged for a tug named the *Mary Ann* to retrieve their stricken shipmates, but in the rough waters she simply was not able to manoeuvre herself close enough to the *Mary Ward*. After considerable effort, and with the tug itself in danger of being either run aground or swamped, her captain had to admit defeat and return to port.

As the tug pulled away, her crew looked over their shoulders and watched in horror as all sense of order was lost aboard the *Mary Ward*. Panic had taken hold. Some of the sailors mutinied and launched the ship's last lifeboat, leaving the passengers and the remaining crew to their fates. It wasn't long before oversized waves began sweeping over the rowboat. It seemed with each crashing wave one sailor was thrown overboard and swept away, lost to the icy embrace of Georgian Bay. Battered relentlessly, the boat finally capsized, spilling the remaining men into the water. They clung desperately to the rowboat's upended hull for a time, but the cold numbed each man's strength as well as his grip until, finally, one by one, they slid below the waves.

When the storm finally lifted, three fishing vessels from Collingwood arrived on the scene and rescued all those remaining aboard the *Mary Ward*. They were cold and shaken, but alive. The eight who had deserted ship had made a deadly and ill-advised choice. Perhaps in their final moments they realized their folly, for it seems their restless souls soon came back to earth.

The tragedy of that night in November 1872 is memorialized in many ways. Milligan's Reef was renamed Mary Ward Shoal in honour of the vessel that now lies in a watery grave six metres deep, while a commemorative plaque honouring the memory of the victims and the brave rescuers can be found at Craigleith Provincial Park.

But it is the ghosts of the eight crewmen who perished aboard the tiny rowboat who continue to provide the most sombre reminder of the maritime disaster. It seems that these men refuse to die. And, as long as they haunt the waters of Georgian Bay, it's unlikely that the *Mary Ward* will be forgotten.

# Further Reading

*Berchem, F. R. *The Yonge Street Story*. Toronto: Natural Heritage, 1996.

Boyer, Robert J. *A Good Town Grew Here: The Story of Bracebridge*. Bracebridge: Oxbow Press, 1975.

*Boyle, Terry. *Haunted Ontario*. Toronto: Polar Bear Press, 1998.

Brown, Ron. *Ontario's Secret Landscapes*. Erin, ON: Boston Mills Press, 1999.

*Coleman, Loren and Patrick Huyghe. *The Field Guide to Bigfoot, Yeti, and Other Mystery Primates Worldwide*. New York: Avon Books, 1999.

Colombo, John Robert. *Mysteries of Ontario*. Toronto: Hounslow Press, 1999.

*Colombo, John Robert. *True Canadian Ghost Stories*. Toronto: Prospero Books, 2003.

Floren, Russell and Andrea Gutsche. *Ghosts of the Bay: A*

## Further Reading

*Guide to the History of Georgian Bay.* Toronto: Lynx Images, 1998.

*Frim, Monica. *Secrets of the Lakes: Stories from the History of Lake Simcoe and Lake Couchiching.* Toronto: Lynx Images, 2002.

Harris, Mark. *Waterfalls of Ontario.* Toronto: Firefly Books, 2003.

Hunter, Andrew Frederick. *A History of Simcoe County.* Barrie: The County Council, 1909.

McDevitt, Francis Vincent and Mary Margaret Munnoch. *Adjala.* Erin: Boston Mills Press, 1993.

*"Murder in Loretto," *Dufferin Advertiser,* 25 February 1892.

Stamp, Robert M. *Early Days in Richmond Hill: A History of the Community to 1930.* Richmond Hill: Richmond Hill Public Library Board, 1991.

Terry, Thomas P. *World Treasure Atlas.* LaCrosse, WI: Speciality Publishing, 1978.

The authors acknowledge that the publications marked with an asterisk (*) are the sources for the quotes within this book.

# Acknowledgments

The authors wish to acknowledge the following sources for their assistance with the manuscript: Jacqueline Stuart, Curator of the Aurora Museum, for the valuable research she uncovered on our behalf; Doreen Nowak of Rosseau, for her personal reminiscences that helped place Mutchinbacker Mills in its proper historical context, and Diane Rotz of Maple for valuable photos and information pertaining to the mills. We appreciate the warm welcome and gracious hospitality of Krista Havenaar, innkeeper and general manager at Inn at the Falls, and indeed to the entire staff who were eager to share their experiences and indulge our curiosity. Ruth Holtz, the reference librarian at the Bracebridge Public Library, offered assistance in tracking down historical facts; and Marie LaRose and the staff at Collingwood Caves Nature Preserve welcomed us with a tour of the folklore-rich setting. Bill Church kindly indulged our interest in the legend of Jesse James' treasure, and the staff of the Dufferin County Museum aided in researching the old tale. Finally, but not least importantly, there are those who related their paranormal personal experiences with us, some of whom asked to remain anonymous for fear of ridicule. Thank you for your trust and courage.

# Further Acknowledgments: Andrew Hind

On a more personal level, Andrew would like to thank his wife, Nicoletta, for understanding his need to immerse himself in the past, and his parents for their unflagging support over 30 odd years. Most of all, he'd like to thank Maria for taking the incredible journey that is writing a book with him, and for giving him the courage to take those frightening first steps in the first place.

# Further Acknowledgments: Maria da Silva

I would like to thank my husband, Henry, and my daughter, Amanda, for all their support through this wonderful experience. I'd also like to thank the Hind family for believing in me. But most of all, thanks to Andrew for seeing something in me that I didn't even think existed.

# Photo Credits

# About the Authors

Andrew Hind is a freelance writer who lives in Bradford, Ontario. His feature articles have appeared in magazines and newspapers across Canada, in the United States, and in England. Andrew developed a passion for history early on, especially for unusual and obscure events that are typically overlooked or quickly forgotten. He hopes, through his writing, to bring these fascinating stories to light for a modern audience.

Maria da Silva has always had a passion for history and ghost stories. Though she came from a country (Portugal) that is full of history and the unknown, she never dreamed that her future would lead her into writing about the forgotten and the unexplained. Maria's work, co-authored with Andrew Hind, has appeared in publications such as *Fate* and *Mystery Magazine.*

Together, Maria and Andrew are researching their next book — about ghost towns of Ontario.

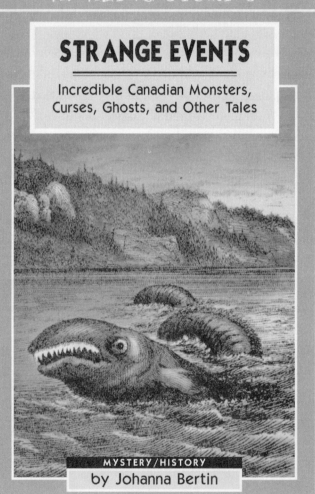

AMAZING STORIES™

# STRANGE EVENTS

Incredible Canadian Monsters,
Curses, Ghosts, and Other Tales

MYSTERY/HISTORY
by Johanna Bertin

# STRANGE EVENTS
## Incredible Canadian Monsters, Curses, Ghosts, and Other Tales

*"Nicholson was shocked when a 'dazzling light and shrieking whistle' came out of nowhere and headed right for his train. Paralysed with fear, he... swore that the passengers in the ghost train's lighted cars had looked directly at him."*

What are the chances of being hit by lightening three times in one lifetime? And then, being hit again after you are dead and buried? This is just one of the incredible legends in this fascinating collection. From ghosts lurking on board mystery ships to the dark and chilling secrets of Niagara's devil's playground, Canada's history has never been so thrilling.

 True stories. Truly Canadian.

ISBN 1-55153-952-7

# STRANGE EVENTS AND MORE
### Canadian Giants, Witches, Wizards, and Other Tales

*"A visiting Presbyterian minister said that he had met [baby] Anna and her mother in a buggy. 'I could not help but stare at this monstrosity and wonder what she had had for breakfast,' he told his friends."*

Myths and legends abound with tales of giants and their feats of exceptional strength, witches and their powers of good and evil, and the miraculous abilities of healers and medicine men. The past comes alive in this selection of stories about extraordinary Canadians who have lived unusual lives.

 True stories. Truly Canadian.

ISBN 1-55153-983-4

# ONTARIO MURDERS
## Mysteries, Scandals, and Dangerous Criminals

*"From an early age, lying came easily to her. Everything she did was a performance, a role she played to create an illusion."*
**From the story of Evelyn Dick**

Six chilling stories of notorious Ontario murders are recounted in this spine-tingling collection. From the pretty but dangerous Evelyn Dick to the mysterious murder of one of the Fathers of Confederation, Thomas D'Darcy McGee, these stories will keep you on the edge of your seat.

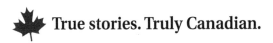 True stories. Truly Canadian.

ISBN 1-55153-951-9

# TORONTO MURDERS
## Mysteries, Crime, and Scandals

*"She said now was the time to kill the
housekeeper, and Mr. Kinnear when
he returns home, and I'll assist you and
you are a coward if you don't do it."*

The history of Toronto is peppered with countless
tales of scandals and murder. This fascinating
collection of crime stories features six chilling
incidents that plagued the city's residents in days
gone by. Exploring deadly love affairs, mysterious
disappearances, and public hangings, these true
accounts will keep you on the edge of your seat.

 True stories. Truly Canadian.

ISBN 1-55439-131-1

# OTHER AMAZING STORIES®

| ISBN | Title | ISBN | Title |
|------|-------|------|-------|
| 1-55439-006-0 | Alexander Graham Bell | 1-55153-944-6 | The Life of a Loyalist |
| 1-55153-978-0 | The Avro Arrow Story | 1-55153-775-3 | Lucy Maud Montgomery |
| 1-55439-025-7 | The Battle of Seven Oaks | 1-55153-787-7 | The Mad Trapper |
| 1-55153-943-8 | The Black Donnellys | 1-55153-953-5 | Moe Norman |
| 1-55153-794-X | Calgary Flames | 1-55439-054-0 | Montreal Canadiens |
| 1-55439-063-X | Canada's Peacekeepers | 1-55153-789-3 | The Mounties |
| 1-55153-966-7 | Canadian Spies | 1-55153-767-2 | The Mystery of the Oak Island Treasure |
| 1-55439-002-8 | Convoys of World War II | | |
| 1-55153-795-8 | D-Day | 1-55153-962-4 | Niagara Daredevils |
| 1-55439-026-5 | Deadly Women of Ontario | 1-55153-951-9 | Ontario Murders |
| 1-55439-004-4 | Disasters Across Canada | 1-55153-790-7 | Ottawa Senators |
| 1-55153-970-5 | Early Voyageurs | 1-55153-945-4 | Pierre Elliot Trudeau |
| 1-55439-027-3 | East Coast Murders | 1-55439-013-3 | Pirates and Privateers |
| 1-55153-798-2 | Edmonton Oilers | 1-55439-050-8 | Prairie Murders |
| 1-55153-996-9 | Emily Carr | 1-55153-991-8 | Rebel Women |
| 1-55153-961-6 | Étienne Brûlé | 1-55439-058-3 | René Lévesque |
| 1-55439-049-4 | Gentleman Train Robber | 1-55153-995-0 | Rescue Dogs |
| 1-55439-053-2 | Gold Fever | 1-55439-003-6 | Rescues on the High Seas |
| 1-55439-057-5 | Great Canadian War Heroes | 1-55153-956-X | Robert Service |
| 1-55153-777-X | Great Cat Stories | 1-55153-799-0 | Roberta Bondar |
| 1-55439-097-4 | Great Centremen | 1-55439-012-5 | Shipwrecks off the East Coast |
| 1-55439-083-4 | Great Defencemen | | |
| 1-55153-946-2 | Great Dog Stories | 1-55439-011-7 | Soapy Smith |
| 1-55439-056-7 | Greatest Grey Cups | 1-55439-028-1 | Spies in our Midst |
| 1-55439-084-2 | Great Goaltenders | 1-55153-971-3 | Stolen Horses |
| 1-55493-082-6 | Great Left Wingers | 1-55439-061-3 | Strange Events of Ontario |
| 1-55439-062-1 | Great Railways of the Canadian West | 1-55153-788-5 | Toronto Maple Leafs |
| | | 1-55439-031-1 | Toronto Murders |
| 1-55439-086-9 | Great Right Wingers | 1-55153-977-2 | Unsung Heroes of the Royal Canadian Air Force |
| 1-55153-942-X | The Halifax Explosion | | |
| 1-55153-958-6 | Hudson's Bay Company Adventures | 1-55153-765-6 | Unsung Heroes of the Royal Canadian Navy |
| 1-55439-047-8 | Inspiring Animal Tales | 1-55153-792-3 | Vancouver Canucks |
| 1-55439-017-6 | Karen Kain | 1-55153-989-6 | Vancouver's Old-Time Scoundrels |
| 1-55439-030-3 | The Last of the Beothuk | | |
| 1-55439-016-8 | Laura Secord | 1-55153-948-9 | The War of 1812 Against the States |
| 1-55439-101-6 | Legendary NHL Coaches | 1-55439-085-0 | Working Miracles |

These titles are available wherever you buy books. Visit our web site at **www.amazingstories.ca**

New **AMAZING STORIES**® titles are published every month.